Copyright © K. Akrill , 1998

All Rights Reserved. No part of this publication may be reproduced, stored in a retrieval system, or transmitted in any form or by any means – electronic, mechanical, photocopying, recording, or otherwise – without prior written permission from the publisher.

Published by Sigma Leisure – an imprint of
Sigma Press, 1 South Oak Lane, Wilmslow, Cheshire SK9 6AR, England.

British Library Cataloguing in Publication Data
A CIP record for this book is available from the British Library.

ISBN: 1-85058-611-X

Typesetting and Design by: Sigma Press, Wilmslow, Cheshire.

Printed by: MFP Design & Print

Cover Design: The Agency, Wilmslow.

Cover illustration: Stuart Fox

Foreword

by David Roberts
– United Kingdom Alliance
and the British Dance Council

Partner dancing has been with us for many centuries and, during the 20th century, it has been the most prolific social pastime. More partnerships were made on the dance floor than anywhere else. Dancing suffered a minor blow with 'The Twist', but once again in the nineties, and into the millennium, partner dancing is once again 'cool'. Every corner of the world now dances together and they are taking their partners in the millions from Beijing to Belarussia and Taiwan to Tasmania. Together dancing also incorporates 'Line Dancing' where, although the dancer is performing solo, because everyone is moving at the same time – everyone in the room becomes your partner.

This book covers every aspect of together dancing, and it shows you clearly and plainly how to make that start into the fabulous world of dancing. The author has a vast experience as a dancing teacher and is recognised as one of the World's leading authorities. Although this book is for fun and fitness it lays the correct foundations should you choose to visit one of the thousands of UKA qualified dance teachers all over the globe and go further for medal tests. You may even be a future competitor representing your Country at the Olympic Games. So: get happy – get healthy – get dancing.

Happy dancing – together!

David Roberts

Company & General Secretary: United Kingdom Alliance of Professional Teachers of Dancing

Director: British Dance Council

Introduction

This publication is intended to serve as a guide to those who wish to reach a level of proficiency in social ballroom and Latin dancing. It does not claim to teach anyone to dance, for only a qualified teacher can do that. It does, however, provide a lucid outline of the figures of Social Waltz, Viennese Waltz, Slow Rhythm Foxtrot, Quick Rhythm Foxtrot (known also as Social Quickstep), Tango, Rumba, Cha Cha Cha, Brazilian Samba, Mambo/Salsa, Merengue, Night Club Swing and trend dances that are popular at this time.

Most of the figures described are those that are recommended by the World Social Dance Committee. The aim of the World Social Dance Committee is to formulate a series of figures that, when learnt, will enable any couple to dance together, regardless of where the individuals were taught, or in which part of the world.

If this book is an aid to you in gaining proficiency in social dancing, then its purpose will have been fully accomplished. It is hoped, however, that those of you who do benefit will be encouraged to continue learning with a qualified dance teacher. Look for the qualifications after a teacher's name - they show that, under examination conditions, he or she has demonstrated ability and competence in the teaching of dancing.

Have fun!

Ken Akrill

Fellow of the United Kingdom Alliance, Dance, Drama and Exercise. Former Fellow and Examiner, International Dance Teachers' Association in Ballroom, Latin American, Classical Sequence and Freestyle.

Contents

What Is Social Dancing?   **1**

The Ballroom Dances   **8**

Waltz   9

Quick Waltz (Viennese Waltz)   25

Social Foxtrot (Slow Rhythm)   33

Social Foxtrot (Quick Rhythm)   46

Tango   53

The Latin Dances   **63**

Merengue   66

Cha Cha Cha   77

Salsa   92

Mambo   99

Rumba   109

Samba   117

Dances for Discos   **128**

Night Club Swing   129

Disco Dances in Lines   140

The Slosh   140

The Macarena   141

Music for Dancing   **143**

What Is Social Dancing?

There is no particular dance that is categorised as a social dance, it is the performance of the dancer who executes the figures in a relaxed style that gives the dance the name 'Social'. The dancers do not wish to be seen as striving for perfection, they are dancing just for the pleasure of dancing. The strict technique that surrounds the dance is not important. What is important is that the couple dancing do so in a relaxed and easy way.

When you begin to practise the dances in this book, the descriptions may at first seem daunting. Don't be put off! Describing just one step takes more words than you would imagine, but with practice you will be doing that step without thinking. Similarly, most of you will have an idea of how to hold your dance partner. Our description is intended for those who are completely new to dancing, and to help you if you feel that your hold could be improved. It's a counsel of perfection which you might find useful, not something to worry about unduly – and it certainly shouldn't stop you from enjoying dancing.

So the important thing is that you actually get on to the dance floor and enjoy yourself. Very few of the other couples will be experts so you won't look foolish, and, with practice, you'll soon be wondering what all the fuss was about.

Before You Start

Before you begin, you need to understand some basic terms that will be used throughout this book. As many of them are used so frequently, we collect them together here for easy reference:

Direction

Most dances travel *around* the floor in an *anticlockwise* direction, keeping reasonably close to the edge of the floor.

Amounts of Turn

The hardest concept to understand when teaching yourself to dance is the amount of turn to dance on certain steps. Dances have an *alignment* – which describes where you are facing, backing, or where the foot is pointing in relation to the room. To describe the amount of turn we divide the room into eight alignments. This means that when you turn from one alignment to another the amount of turn is measured in eighths. Eight eighths are, therefore, a complete turn, either to the right or left.

The problem is that this concept does not cover the *direction* in which the foot moves when making a turn. Using the analogy of a clock face will help you to make the right amount of a turn. Assuming that the room you are in is of a normal shape – having four walls and four corners, so eight alignments – decide which wall will be your 12 o'clock direction. When facing this wall, you are on the **Line of Dance**. If you take one-eighth of a turn at a time, this is how you should progress:

❋ Turn to the right (clockwise) to face the first corner of the room (approximately 2 o'clock) and you are now *Facing diagonally to Wall*

❋ Turn to your second wall (3 o'clock) and you are *Facing Wall*

❋ Continuing to turn, your second corner in the room (4 o'clock) is *Facing Diagonally to Wall against Line of Dance*

❋ Turning once again brings you to your third wall (6 o'clock) and *Facing against the Line of Dance*

❋ A further turn brings you to your third corner (8 o'clock) and you are now *Facing diagonally to Centre against Line of Dance*

❋ Your fourth wall (9 o'clock) brings you to *Facing Centre*

❋ Finally, your fourth corner (10 o'clock) is *Facing diagonally to Centre*

And that's it! Those are the only alignments you need to know.

No	Alignments Turning Clockwise	Clockface
1.	Line of Dance.	12 o'clock.
2.	Diagonally to Wall.	2 o'clock.
3.	Wall.	3 o'clock.
4.	Diagonally to Wall against Line of Dance.	4 o'clock.
5.	Against Line of Dance.	6 o'clock.
6.	Diagonally to Centre against Line of Dance.	8 o'clock.
7.	Centre.	9 o'clock.
8.	Diagonally to Centre.	10 o'clock.

These alignments can be given as *facing, backing* or *pointing*.

Terms You Should Know

The Hold

In most social dances we use what is termed the "close hold". Stand in an upright position, feet together, sides of the body braced. Raise the arms so that there is a slight downward slope from the shoulders to the elbows. The man then takes the lady's right hand, palm to palm, into his left hand, her fingers being held between the first finger and thumb with the man's fingers closed around the lady's right hand. The joined hands are then raised approximately to the height of the man's left ear with the joined hands held to the side. The man places his right hand underneath the lady's left shoulder blade with the fingers neatly grouped together and pointing diagonally downwards. The finger tips of the right hand are just touching the lady's spine. The lady places her left hand on the man's upper right forearm, her fingers neatly grouped just below his right shoulder. The lady's left arm will follow, as close as possible, the man's right arm. The man's left arm will slope upwards showing an unbroken line from the left elbow to the knuckles of the man's left hand.

Foot Position

This describes the position of one foot in relation to the other at the end of a step (that is, when most of the weight is received on that foot).

Example: using the right foot in relation to the left foot.

Facing **Line of Dance** (12 o'clock). Having stepped forward with the **left foot**, move the **right foot** directly to the side, towards the **Wall** (3 o'clock). We can now say that the **right foot** is to the side of the **left foot**.

Foot Position and Direction

Example: a Foot Position with a Direction, using steps 1 and 2 of the man's Natural Turn in the Waltz.

Preparatory Position: Facing diagonally to Wall (2 o'clock)

Step 1. **Right foot** forward, diagonally to Wall, turning body to right.

Step 2. **Left foot** to side, moving diagonally to Wall, continue to turn to end backing diagonally to Centre.

Analysis   Step 1. At the end of the step, the **right foot** is facing in the same direction as the body, that is, facing diagonally to Wall.

Step 2. The left foot moves *forward*, diagonally to Wall, while you continue to turn on the right foot to finish with the left foot to the side. At the end of the step the body having continued to turn is *backing* diagonally to Centre.

Body and Foot Alignments

Describe the direction in which the moving foot (or feet) is **Pointing**, *or where the body is* **Facing** *or* **Backing**, *in relation to the room.* The alignment is always given at the end of the step.

Example: a Facing Alignment, using step 1 of the man's Natural Turn in the Waltz.

Preparatory Position: Facing diagonally to Wall (2 o'clock)

Step 1. **Right foot** forward, diagonally to Wall.

Analysis   Step 1. At the end of the step, the **right foot** and the **body** are facing in the same direction.

Example: a Pointing Alignment, using step 2 of the lady's Natural Turn in the Waltz.

Preparatory Position: Backing diagonally to Wall (2 o'clock)

Step 2. **Right foot** to the side, moving diagonally to Wall, continue to turn to end with the **right foot** *pointing* to Line of Dance.

Analysis   Step 2. At the end of the step, the **right foot** is pointing to Line of Dance, but the **body is facing diagonally to Centre**. When the body and foot have different alignments, we always refer to the foot alignment.

The body will continue to turn during the closing of the **left foot** to the **right foot** on step 3.

Example: a Backing Alignment, using step 3 of the man's Natural Turn in the Waltz.

Preparatory Position: Backing diagonally to Centre (10 o'clock)

Step 3. Close **right foot to left foot**, still turning, to end *backing* Line of Dance.

Analysis   At the end of the step, the feet and body are backing the Line of Dance.

Foot and Body Turn

Example turns

Again, using the analogy of a clock face, amounts of turn are easy to understand. Imagine you are standing in the centre of a clock face, facing 12.o'clock.

Turning clockwise: (turning to the right)

Start Clock	Finish Clock	Amount of Turn	Body Alignment
12 o'clock.	2 o'clock.	⅛ to right.	Facing diagonally to Wall.
12 o'clock.	3 o'clock.	¼ to right.	Facing Wall.
12 o'clock.	4 o'clock.	⅜ to right.	Facing diagonally to Wall against Line of Dance.
12 o'clock.	6 o'clock.	½ to right.	Facing against Line of Dance.
12 o'clock.	8 o'clock.	⅝ to right.	Facing diagonally to Centre against Line of Dance.
12 o'clock.	9 o'clock.	¾ to right.	Facing Centre.
12 o'clock.	10 o'clock.	⅞ to right.	Facing diagonally to Centre.
12 o'clock.	12 o'clock.	Full turn.	Facing Line of Dance.

Turning anti-clockwise: (turning to the left)

Start Clock	Finish Clock	Amount of Turn	Body Alignment
12 o'clock.	10 o'clock.	⅛ to left.	Facing diagonally to Centre.
12 o'clock.	9 o'clock.	¼ to left.	Facing Centre.
12 o'clock.	8 o'clock.	⅜ to left.	Facing diagonally to Centre against Line of Dance.
12 o'clock.	6 o'clock.	½ to left.	Facing against Line of Dance.
12 o'clock.	4 o'clock.	⅝ to left.	Facing diagonally to Wall against Line of Dance.
12 o'clock.	3 o'clock.	¾ to left.	Facing Wall.
12 o'clock.	2 o'clock.	⅞ to left.	Facing diagonally to Wall.
12 o'clock.	12 o'clock.	Full turn.	Facing Line of Dance.

Direction of the moving foot in turns

When dancing into a turn, the direction of the moving foot is sometimes different from that of the body. An example would be the **Natural Turn** in the Waltz.

Preparatory Position: Facing diagonally to Wall (2 o'clock)

Step 1. **Right foot** forward, turning the body to the right.

Step 2. **Left foot** to the side, continue to turn a ¼ turn to the right.

Analysis   The body turns to face **diagonally to Wall against Line of Dance** (4 o'clock), but the left foot is moved **diagonally to Wall** (2 o'clock), to finish with the **left foot** to the side. The turn is initiated in the body and then continued through the feet, which results in the feet swivelling clockwise.

Remembering that each section of the clock represents an eighth of a turn, consult the clock chart and you will see that turning from 2 o'clock to 4 o'clock equals two eighths or a ¼ turn to the right.

A further example would be:

Preparatory Position: Backing diagonally to Wall (2 o'clock)

Step 1. Left foot back, turning the body to the right.

Step 2. **Right foot** to side, foot pointing to Line of Dance.

Analysis   On step two the body turns to face diagonally to Centre (10 o'clock), but the **right foot** is moved diagonally to Wall (2 o'clock), to finish with the **right foot** to the side, pointing to Line of Dance (12 o'clock.)

The turn is initiated in the body, on step one, and then the turn is continued by moving the **right foot** to point to the Line of Dance. The body will then line up with the foot to face Line of Dance on the closing step. Notice that no foot swivelling occurs.

Directions are not given for closing steps as these are self explanatory.

Footwork

This term describes the part or parts of the foot, or feet, that make contact with the floor while dancing. In the progressive dances you will find that the correct footwork not only improves your balance, but also your poise.

Example: the footwork, heel flat, on a Forward Walk, using step 1 of the man's Natural Turn in the Waltz.

Preparatory Position: Facing diagonally to Wall (2 o'clock)

Step 1. **Right foot** forward, turning the body to the right. Heel flat.

Analysis   The **right foot** moves forward with the heel skimming the floor to arrive on the heel with the toes off the floor. Transferring the weight of the body on to the **right foot**, lower the **right foot** flat to the floor.

Example: the footwork, ball flat, on a Backward Walk, using step 1 of the lady's Natural Turn in the Waltz.

Preparatory Position: Backing diagonally to Wall (2 o'clock)

Analysis   The **left foot** moves backwards with the toes skimming the floor. Transferring the weight of the body on to the **left foot**, lower the **left foot** flat to the floor.

Example: the footwork, ball, on a Side Step, using step 2 of the man's Natural Turn in the Waltz.
Preparatory Position: Facing diagonally to Wall (2 o'clock)

Analysis   The **left foot** moves to the side on the ball of the foot with the heel raised from the floor. When transferring the weight of the body on to the **left foot**, ensure that the **left foot** does not lower flat to the floor.

Example: the footwork, ball flat, on a Closing Step, using step 3 of the lady's Natural Turn in the Waltz.
Preparatory Position: Foot pointing to Line of Dance (12 o'clock)

Analysis   The **left foot** closes to the **right foot** with the toes in light contact with the floor. When the feet are together, transfer the weight of the body on to the closing foot, lowering the **left foot** flat to the floor.

Example: The Forward Walk on the Right Foot

The **right foot** commences to move forward on the ball of the foot, but transfers to the heel as it moves. When the heel of the **right foot** passes the toes of the **left foot**, the heel of the supporting **left foot** is released from the floor. The **right foot** continues to move forward with the heel skimming the floor, so that at the full extent of the stride the body weight is equally divided between the heel of the **right foot** and the ball of the **left foot**. The **right foot** lowers flat to the floor as the **left foot** closes to the **right foot** with slight pressure on the ball of foot.

Example: The Backward Walk on the Left Foot

The **left foot** commences to move back first on the ball of foot then transfers to the toes. When the toes of the **left foot** have passed the heel of the **right foot**, the toes of the **right foot** are released from the floor. The **left foot** continues to move back, lowering to the ball of foot at the full extent of the stride. The body weight is now equally divided between the heel of the **right foot** and the ball of the **left foot**. The **right foot** commences to move back with slight pressure to the floor through the heel then into the ball of foot. When the **right foot** draws level with the **left foot**, the left heel is lowered to the floor with the **right foot** on the ball of the foot, without weight.

How to Study the Figures

❋ First learn the Foot Position and Direction of the feet, incorporating the amounts of turn, if any.

❋ *Apply the footwork.*

❋ Practise first without the music, then with the music.

The Ballroom Dances

The ballroom dances include the waltz, foxtrot and tango. Of these, the waltz is probably the one that you will encounter most often. The steps and techniques in the waltz are given far more coverage than any other dance in this book so that you have a thorough grasp of dance fundamentals. What you learn in the waltz. You can apply in other dances. So, it's time to take your partner and learn to dance – together!

Waltz

Time signature: ¾; three beats to the bar.

Rhythm: The first beat in each bar is accented. Count 1-2-3. There are no Slows or Quicks.

Tempo: Music should be played at about 30 to 32 bars per minute. (90 – 96mm.)

Of all the social dances, the waltz remains the most popular. It will be played at any function which you attend so you're certain to have opportunities to use your new skills, and, if for no other reason, it's worth learning so that you don't have to sit out the "last waltz"! It is a gentle, graceful dance which suits a variety of contemporary music, and its slow to moderate tempo makes it an ideal introduction to partner dancing.

About the dance

When starting to learn the figures in the Waltz you should first of all learn the Forward Changes. When you have mastered the Forward Changes, start facing the Line of Dance, and dance a series of Change Steps, starting first with the Forward Change on the left foot, followed by a Forward Change on the right foot.

The amalgamation of Change Steps should be danced in a straight line down the side of the room, moving in an anti-clockwise direction. Having mastered the Change Steps and acquired the necessary footwork (for without this the turns will be more difficult to master, and the footwork of the Waltz is so consistent and easy that it need not intimidate the non-dancer), proceed then to learn the Natural and Reverse Squares. It is easier to practise first without actually making any turn – that is dancing "Forward, side, close, back, side, close," and making a square without altering the direction. You can then practise these squares making a little turn until you can accomplish, with ease, the amount of turn that is required. When the turns of the Squares have been mastered you can repeat this process for learning the Natural and Reverse Turns.

At a corner, only a Natural Turn or Hesitation Turn is used. It can be arranged in two ways: either dance two complete Natural Turns, making a ½ turn on the first Natural Turn, then only a ¼ turn over steps 1 to 3 of the second Natural Turn. Make no turn over steps 4 to 6, to end facing the new Line of Dance. Alternatively, you can dance a Hesitation Change, making a ¼ (or ⅜) turn to the right over steps 4 to 6. This amount of turn will end you facing the new Line of Dance (¼), or diagonally to the Wall of the new Line of Dance (⅜).

The Forward Changes

The basis of the Waltz is built on Change Steps. Briefly, a Change Step is a walk followed by a side, close and is so-named because a change of weight occurs on each foot close. Although non-dancers can amalgamate the Changes (which will allow them to progress around the room), the main use of the Change Step is to link together two turns. There are two Forward Changes: the **Left Foot**

Change is used after a Reverse Turn and a **Right Foot Change** is used after a Natural Turn.

Forward Change (Left foot)

This is normally used after a Reverse Turn to a Natural Turn.

Man's steps

Preparatory Position: Start facing diagonally to Wall, weight on the **right foot**, in Close Hold. End facing diagonally to Wall.

Step	Foot Position and Direction	Turn	Footwork	Body Alignment
1.	**Left foot** forward, diagonally to Wall.	Nil.	Heel flat.	Facing diagonally to Wall.
2.	**Right foot** to side, moving diagonally to Wall against Line of Dance.	Nil.	Ball.	Facing diagonally to Wall.
3.	Close **left foot** to **right foot**.	Nil.	Ball flat.	Facing diagonally to Wall.

Rhythm: 1– 2 – 3
Calling Cues: Forward – Side – Close

Lady's steps

Preparatory Position: Start backing diagonally to Wall, weight on the **left foot**, in Close Hold. End backing diagonally to Wall.

Step	Foot Position and Direction	Turn	Footwork	Body Alignment
1.	**Right foot** back, diagonally to Wall.	Nil.	Ball flat.	Backing diagonally to Wall.
2.	**Left foot** to side, moving diagonally to Wall against Line of Dance.	Nil.	Ball.	Backing diagonally to Wall.
3.	Close **right foot** to **left foot**.	Nil.	Ball flat.	Backing diagonally to Wall.

Rhythm: 1 – 2 – 3
Calling Cues: Back – Side – Close

Forward Change (Right foot):

Normally used from a Natural Turn to a Reverse Turn.

Man's steps

Preparatory Position: Start facing diagonally to Centre, weight on the **left foot**, in Close Hold. End facing diagonally to Centre.

Step	Foot Position and Direction	Turn	Footwork	Body Alignment
1.	**Right foot** forward, diagonally to Centre.	Nil.	Heel flat.	Facing diagonally to Centre.
2.	**Left foot** to side, moving diagonally to Centre against Line of Dance.	Nil.	Ball.	Facing diagonally to Centre.
3.	Close **right foot** to **left foot**.	Nil.	Ball flat.	Facing diagonally to Centre.

Rhythm: 1 – 2 – 3
Calling Cues: Forward – Side – Close

Lady's steps

Preparatory Position: Start backing diagonally to Centre, weight on the **right foot**, in Close Hold. End backing diagonally to Centre.

Step	Foot Position and Direction	Turn	Footwork	Body Alignment
1.	**Left foot** back, diagonally to Centre.	Nil.	Ball flat.	Backing diagonally to Centre.
2.	**Right foot** to side, diagonally to Centre against Line of Dance.	Nil.	Ball.	Backing diagonally to Centre.
3.	Close **left foot** to **right foot**.	Nil.	Ball flat.	Backing diagonally to Centre.

Rhythm: 1 – 2 – 3
Calling Cues: Back – Side – Close

Reverse Square:

The Squares are useful figures in giving the man and lady practice in stepping forward and back.

Man's steps

Preparatory Position: Start facing diagonally to Wall, weight on the **right foot**, in Close Hold. End facing diagonally to Centre.

Step	Foot Position and Direction	Turn	Footwork	Body Alignment
1.	Left foot forward, diagonally to Wall.	Body turn to left.	Heel flat.	Facing diagonally to Wall.
2.	**Right foot** to the side, moving to Wall.	Continue to turn.	Ball.	Backing against Line of Dance.
3.	Close **left foot** to **right foot**.	⅛ to left, over steps 1-3.	Ball flat.	Backing against Line of Dance.
4.	**Right foot** back, against Line of Dance.	Body turn to left.	Ball flat.	Backing against Line of Dance.
5.	Left foot to the side, diagonally to Centre against Line of Dance.	Continue to turn.	Ball.	Facing diagonally to Centre.
6.	Close **right foot** to **left foot**.	⅛ to left, over steps 4-6.	Ball flat.	Facing diagonally to Centre.

Rhythm: 1 – 2 – 3 – 1 – 2 – 3
Calling Cues: Forward – Side – Close – Back – Side – Close

Lady's steps

Preparatory Position: Start backing diagonally to Wall, weight on the **left foot**, in Close Hold. End backing diagonally to Centre.

Step	Foot Position and Direction	Turn	Footwork	Body Alignment
1.	**Right foot** back, diagonally to Wall.	Body turn to left.	Ball flat.	Backing diagonally to Wall.
2.	Left foot to the side, moving to Wall.	Continue to turn.	Ball.	Facing against Line of Dance.

3.	Close **right foot** to **left foot**.	⅛ to left, over steps 1-3.	Ball flat.	Facing against Line of Dance.
4.	Left foot forward, against Line of Dance.	Body turn to left.	Heel flat.	Facing against Line of Dance.
5.	**Right foot** to the side, moving diagonally to Centre against Line of Dance.	Continue to turn.	Ball.	Backing diagonally to Centre.
6.	Close **left foot** to **right foot**.	⅛ to left, over steps 4-6.	Ball flat.	Backing diagonally to Centre.

Rhythm: 1 – 2 – 3 – 1 – 2 – 3
Calling Cues: Back – Side – Close – Forward – Side – Close

Natural Square

Man's steps

Preparatory Position: Start facing diagonally to Centre, weight on the **left foot**, in Close Hold. End facing diagonally to Wall.

Step	Foot Position and Direction	Turn	Footwork	Body Alignment
1.	**Right foot** forward, diagonally to Centre.	Body turn to right.	Heel flat.	Facing diagonally to Centre.
2.	**Left foot** to the side, moving to Centre.	Continue to turn.	Ball.	Backing against Line of Dance.
3.	Close **right foot** to **left foot**.	⅛ to right, over steps 1-3.	Ball flat.	Backing against Line of Dance.
4.	**Left foot** back, against Line of Dance.	Body turn to right.	Ball flat.	Backing against Line of Dance.
5.	**Right foot** to the side, moving diagonally to Wall against Line of Dance.	Continue to turn.	Ball.	Facing diagonally to Wall.
6.	Close **left foot** to **right foot**.	⅛ to right, over steps 4-6.	Ball flat.	Facing diagonally to Wall.

Rhythm: 1 – 2 – 3 – 1 – 2 – 3
Calling Cues: Forward – Side – Close – Back – Side – Close

Lady's steps

Preparatory Position: Start backing diagonally to Centre, weight on the **right foot**, in Close Hold. End backing diagonally to Wall.

Step	Foot Position and Direction	Turn	Footwork	Body Alignment
1.	**Left foot** back, diagonally to Centre.	Body turn to right.	Ball flat.	Backing diagonally to Centre.
2.	**Right foot** to the side, moving to Centre.	Continue to turn.	Ball.	Facing against Line of Dance.
3.	Close **left foot** to **right foot**.	⅛ to right, over steps 1-3.	Ball flat.	Facing against Line of Dance.
4.	**Right foot** forward, against Line of Dance.	Body turn to right.	Heel flat.	Facing against Line of Dance.
5.	**Left foot** to the side, diagonally to Wall against Line of Dance.	Continue to turn.	Ball.	Backing diagonally to Wall.
6.	Close **right foot** to **left foot**.	⅛ to right, over steps 4-6.	Ball flat.	Backing diagonally to Wall.

Rhythm: 1 – 2 – 3 – 1 – 2 – 3
Calling Cues: Back – Side – Close – Forward – Side – Close

Backward Passing Change: Natural to Reverse

Man's steps

Preparatory Position: Start facing diagonally to Wall, weight on the **left foot**, in Close Hold. End facing diagonally to Wall.

Step	Foot Position and Direction	Turn	Footwork	Body Alignment
1.	**Right foot** forward, diagonally to Wall.	Body turn to right.	Heel flat.	Facing diagonally to Wall.
2.	**Left foot** to side, along Line of Dance.	Continue to turn.	Ball.	Backing Centre.
3.	Close **right foot** to **left foot**.	¼ to right, over steps 1-3.	Ball flat.	Backing diagonally to Centre.

4.	**Left foot** back, diagonally to Centre.	Nil.	Ball flat.	Backing diagonally to Centre.
5.	**Right foot** back, diagonally to Centre.	Nil.	Ball.	Backing diagonally to Centre.
6.	**Left foot** back, diagonally to Centre.	Nil.	Ball flat.	Backing diagonally to Centre.
7.	**Right foot** back, diagonally to Centre.	Body turn to left.	Ball flat.	Backing diagonally to Centre.
8.	**Left foot** to side, along Line of Dance.	Continue to turn.	Ball.	Foot pointing diagonally to Wall.
9.	Close **right foot** to **left foot**.	¼ to left, over steps 7-9.	Ball flat.	Facing diagonally to Wall.

Rhythm: 1 – 2 – 3 – 1 – 2 – 3 – 1 – 2 – 3
Calling Cues: Forward – Turn – Close – Back – Back – Back – Back – Turn – Close

Lady's steps

Preparatory Position: Start backing diagonally to Wall, weight on the **right foot**, in Close Hold. End backing diagonally to Wall.

Step	Foot Position and Direction	Turn	Footwork	Body Alignment
1.	**Left foot** back, diagonally to Wall.	Body turn to right.	Ball flat.	Backing diagonally to Wall.
2.	**Right foot** to side, along Line of Dance.	Continue to turn.	Ball.	Foot pointing diagonally to Centre.
3.	Close **left foot** to **right foot**.	¼ to right, over steps 1-3.	Ball flat.	Facing diagonally to Centre.
4.	**Right foot** forward, diagonally to Centre.	Nil.	Heel flat.	Facing diagonally to Centre.
5.	**Left foot** forward, diagonally to Centre.	Nil.	Ball.	Facing diagonally to Centre.

6.	**Right foot** forward, diagonally to Centre.	Nil.	Ball flat.	Facing diagonally to Centre.
7.	**Left foot** forward, diagonally to Centre.	Body turn to left.	Heel flat.	Facing diagonally to Centre.
8.	**Right foot** to side, along Line of Dance.	Continue to turn.	Ball.	Backing Wall.
9.	Close **left foot** to **right foot**.	¼ to left, over steps 7-9.	Ball flat.	Backing diagonally to Wall.

Rhythm: 1 – 2 – 3 – 1 – 2 – 3 – 1 – 2 – 3
Calling Cues: Back – Turn – Close – Forward – Forward – Forward – Forward – Turn – Close
Note: The man can turn a ⅛ turn to the right over steps 4 to 6, to end backing Line of Dance. Also steps 4 to 6 can be replaced by steps 4 to 6 of the Natural Square, commenced and ended backing diagonally to Centre.

Backward Passing Change: Reverse to Natural

Man's steps

Preparatory Position: Start facing diagonally to Centre, weight on **right foot**, in Close Hold. End facing diagonally to Centre.

Step	Foot Position and Direction	Turn	Footwork	Body Alignment
1.	**Left foot** forward, diagonally to Centre.	Body turn to left.	Heel flat.	Facing diagonally to Centre.
2.	**Right foot** to side, along Line of Dance.	Continue to turn.	Ball.	Backing Wall.
3.	Close **left foot** to **right foot**.	¼ to left, over steps 1-3.	Ball flat.	Backing diagonally to Wall.
4.	**Right foot** back, diagonally to Wall.	Nil.	Ball flat.	Backing diagonally to Wall.
5.	**Left foot** back, diagonally to Wall.	Nil.	Ball.	Backing diagonally to Wall.
6.	**Right foot** back, diagonally to Wall.	Nil.	Ball flat.	Backing diagonally to Wall.

7.	**Left foot** back, diagonally to Wall.	Body turn to right.	Ball flat.	Backing diagonally to Wall.
8.	**Right foot** to side, along Line of Dance.	Continue to turn.	Ball.	Foot pointing diagonally to Centre.
9.	Close **left foot** to **right foot**.	¼ to right, over steps 7-9.	Ball flat.	Facing diagonally to Centre.

Rhythm: 1 – 2 – 3 – 1 – 2 – 3 – 1 – 2 – 3
Calling Cues: Forward – Turn – Close – Back – Back – Back – Back – Turn – Close

Lady's steps

Preparatory Position: Start backing diagonally to Centre, weight on **left foot**, in Close Hold. End backing diagonally to Centre.

Step	Foot Position and Direction	Turn	Footwork	Body Alignment
1.	**Right foot** back, diagonally to Centre.	Body turn to left.	Ball flat.	Backing diagonally to Centre.
2.	**Left foot** to side, along Line of Dance.	Continue to turn.	Ball.	Foot pointing diagonally to Wall.
3.	Close **right foot** to **left foot**.	¼ to left, over steps 1-3.	Ball flat.	Facing diagonally to Wall.
4.	**Left foot** forward, diagonally to Wall.	Nil.	Heel flat.	Facing diagonally to Wall.
5.	**Right foot** forward, diagonally to Wall.	Nil.	Ball.	Facing diagonally to Wall.
6.	**Left foot** forward, diagonally to Wall.	Nil.	Ball flat.	Facing diagonally to Wall.
7.	**Right foot** forward, diagonally to Wall.	Body turn to right.	Heel flat.	Facing diagonally to Wall.

Step	Foot Position and Direction	Turn	Footwork	Body Alignment
8.	**Left foot** to side, along Line of Dance.	Continue to turn.	Ball.	Backing Centre.
9.	Close **right foot** to **left foot**.	¼ to right, over steps 7-9.	Ball flat.	Backing diagonally to Centre.

Rhythm: 1 – 2 – 3 – 1 – 2 – 3 – 1 – 2 – 3
Calling Cues: Back – Turn – Close – Forward – Forward – Forward – Forward – Turn – Close
Note: The man can turn a ⅛ turn to the left over steps 4 to 6, to end backing Line of Dance. Also steps 4 to 6 can be replaced by steps 4 to 6 of the Reverse Square, commenced and ended backing diagonally to Wall.

Natural Turn (also known as the Right Turn):

Man's steps

Preparatory Position: Start facing diagonally to Wall, weight on **left foot**, in Close Hold. End facing diagonally to Centre.

Step	Foot Position and Direction	Turn	Footwork	Body Alignment
1.	**Right foot** forward, diagonally to Wall, between partner's feet.	Body turn to right.	Heel flat.	Facing diagonally to Wall.
2.	**Left foot** to the side, diagonally to Wall.	Continue to turn.	Ball.	Backing diagonally to Centre.
3.	Close **right foot** to **left foot**.	⅜ to right, over steps 1-3.	Ball flat.	Backing Line of Dance.
4.	**Left foot** to the side and slightly back, diagonally to Wall.	Body turn to right.	Ball flat.	Backing Line of Dance.
5.	**Right foot** to the side, along Line of Dance.	Continue to turn.	Ball.	Foot pointing diagonally to Centre.
6.	Close **left foot** to **right foot**.	⅜ to right, over steps 4-6.	Ball flat.	Facing diagonally to Centre.

Rhythm: 1 – 2 – 3 – 1 – 2 – 3
Calling Cues: Forward – Turn – Close – Back – Turn – Close

Lady's steps

Preparatory Position: Start backing diagonally to Wall, weight on **right foot**, in Close Hold. End backing diagonally to Centre.

Step	Foot Position and Direction	Turn	Footwork	Body Alignment
1.	**Left foot** to the side and slightly back, to Wall.	Body turn to right.	Ball flat.	Backing diagonally to Wall.
2.	**Right foot** to the side, diagonally to Wall.	Continue to turn.	Ball.	Foot pointing to Line of Dance.
3.	Close **left foot** to **right foot**.	⅜ to right, over steps 1-3.	Ball flat.	Facing Line of Dance.
4.	**Right foot** forward, down Line of Dance, between partner's feet.	Body turn to right.	Heel flat.	Facing Line of Dance.
5.	**Left foot** to the side, along Line of Dance.	Continue to turn.	Ball.	Backing Centre.
6.	Close **right foot** to **left foot**.	⅜ to right, over steps 4-6.	Ball flat.	Backing diagonally to Centre.

Rhythm: 1 – 2 – 3 – 1 – 2 – 3
Calling Cues: Back – Turn – Close – Forward – Turn – Close

The Reverse Turn (also known as the Left Turn):

Man's steps

Preparatory Position: Start facing diagonally to Centre, weight on the **right foot**, in Close Hold. End facing diagonally to Wall.

Step	Foot Position and Direction	Turn	Footwork	Body Alignment
1.	**Left foot** forward, diagonally to Centre.	Body turn to left.	Heel flat.	Facing diagonally to Centre.
2.	**Right foot** to the side, diagonally to Centre.	Continue to turn.	Ball.	Backing diagonally to Wall.
3.	Close **left foot** to **right foot**.	⅜ to left, over steps 1-3.	Ball flat.	Backing Line of Dance.

Step	Foot Position and Direction	Turn	Footwork	Body Alignment
4.	**Right foot** to side and slightly back, diagonally to Centre.	Body turn to left.	Ball flat.	Backing Line of Dance.
5.	**Left foot** to the side, along Line of Dance.	Continue to turn.	Ball.	Foot pointing diagonally to Wall.
6.	Close **right foot** to left foot.	⅜ to left, over steps 4-6.	Ball flat.	Facing diagonally to Wall.

Rhythm: 1 – 2 – 3 – 1 – 2 – 3
Calling Cues: Forward – Turn – Close – Back – Turn – Close

Lady's steps

Preparatory Position: Start backing diagonally to Centre, weight on the **left foot**, in Close Hold. End backing diagonally to Wall.

Step	Foot Position and Direction	Turn	Footwork	Body Alignment
1.	**Right foot** to side and slightly back, to Centre.	Body turn to left.	Ball flat.	Backing diagonally to Centre.
2.	**Left foot** to the side, diagonally to Centre.	Continue to turn.	Ball.	Foot pointing to Line of Dance.
3.	Close **right foot** to left foot.	⅜ to left, over steps 1-3.	Ball flat.	Facing Line of Dance.
4.	**Left foot** forward, down Line of Dance, between partner's feet.	Body turn to left.	Heel flat.	Facing Line of Dance.
5.	**Right foot** to the side, along Line of Dance.	Continue to turn.	Ball.	Backing Wall.
6.	Close **Left foot** to right foot.	⅜ to left, over steps 4-6.	Ball flat.	Backing diagonally to Wall.

Rhythm: 1 – 2 – 3 – 1 – 2 – 3
Calling Cues: Back – Turn – Close – Forward – Turn – Close

R104,158/793.33

Hesitation Change:

Man's steps

Preparatory Position: Start facing diagonally to Wall, weight on the **left foot**, in Close Hold. End facing diagonally to Centre.

Step	Foot Position and Direction	Turn	Footwork	Body Alignment
1.	**Right foot** forward, diagonally to Wall, between partner's feet.	Body turn to right.	Heel flat.	Facing diagonally to Wall.
2.	**Left foot** to the side, diagonally to Wall.	Continue to turn.	Ball.	Backing diagonally to Centre.
3.	Close **right foot** to **left foot**.	⅜ to right, over steps 1-3.	Ball flat.	Backing Line of Dance.
4.	**Left foot** to the side and slightly back, diagonally to Wall.	Body turn to right.	Ball flat.	Backing Line of Dance.
5.	**Right foot** to the side, along Line of Dance.	Continue to turn.	Ball flat.	Foot pointing diagonally to Centre.
6.	Close **left foot** to **right foot**, without weight.	⅜ to right, over steps 4-6.	Ball.	Facing diagonally to Centre.

Rhythm: 1 – 2 – 3 – 1 – 2 – 3
Calling Cues: Forward – Turn – Close – Back – Turn – Close
Note: The footwork of step 5 is Ball flat. This helps to keep the balance when closing without a weight change on step 6.

Lady's steps

Preparatory Position: Start backing diagonally to Wall, weight on the **left foot**, in Close Hold. End backing diagonally to Centre.

Step	Foot Position and Direction	Turn	Footwork	Body Alignment
1.	**Left foot** to the side and slightly back, to Wall.	Body turn to right.	Ball flat.	Backing diagonally to Wall.
2.	**Right foot** to the side, diagonally to Wall.	Continue to turn.	Ball.	Foot pointing to Line of Dance.

3.	Close **left foot** to **right foot**.	⅜ to right, over steps 1-3.	Ball flat.	Facing Line of Dance.
4.	**Right foot** forward, down Line of Dance, between partner's feet.	Body turn to right.	Heel flat.	Facing Line of Dance.
5.	**Left foot** to the side, along Line of Dance.	⅜ to right, over steps 4-5.	Ball flat.	Backing diagonally to Centre.
6.	Close **right foot** to **left foot**, without weight.	Nil.	Ball.	Backing diagonally to Centre.

Rhythm: 1 – 2 – 3 – 1 – 2 – 3
Calling Cues: Back – Turn – Close – Forward – Turn – Close
Note: The footwork of step 5 is Ball flat. This helps to keep the balance when closing without a weight change on step 6. Note also that the lady completes her turn between steps 4 and 5.

Precedes and Follows

It is useful to know which figures can precede and follow any particular figure. The following suggestions will be helpful when you decide to put together your own choreography. Remember that in Social dancing less progression is made around the room. Dancing using the alignment on a figure is not too important, providing you are not a hindrance to other dancers. *Any turn to the right that finishes at a corner can be immediately followed with another right turn.*

Forward Change (Left foot)
Before: Forward Change (**Right foot**), Reverse Square, Backward Passing Change (Natural to Reverse), Reverse Turn, and Hesitation Change.
After: Forward Change (**Right foot**), Natural Square, Backward Passing Change (Natural to Reverse), Natural Turn and Hesitation Change.

Forward Change (Right foot)
Before: Forward Change (**Left foot**), Natural Square, Backward Passing Change (Reverse to Natural) and Natural Turn.
After: Forward Change (**Left foot**), Reverse Square, Backward Passing Change (Reverse to Natural) and Reverse Turn.

Reverse Square
Before: Forward Change (**Right foot**), Reverse Square, Backward Passing Change (Natural to Reverse), Reverse Turn and Hesitation Change.
After: Forward Change (**Left foot**), Reverse Square, Backward Passing Change (Reverse to Natural) and Reverse Turn.

Natural Square
Before: Forward Change (**Left foot**), Natural Square, Backward Passing Change (Reverse to Natural) and Right Turn.

After: Forward Change (**Right foot**), Natural Square, Backward Passing Change (Natural to Reverse), Natural Turn and Hesitation Change.

Backward Passing Change: Natural to Reverse
Before: Forward Change (**Left foot**), Natural Square, Natural Turn (at a corner).
After: Forward Change (**Left foot**), Reverse Square and Reverse Turn.

Backward Passing Change: Reverse to Natural
Before: Forward Change (**Right foot**), Reverse Square and Reverse Turn.
After: Forward Change (**Right foot**), Natural Square, Natural Turn and Hesitation Change.

Natural Turn
Before: Forward Change (**Left foot**), Natural Square, Backward Passing Change (Reverse to Natural) and Natural Turn.
After: Forward Change (**Right foot**), Natural Square, Natural Turn and Hesitation Change.

Reverse Turn
Before: Forward Change (**Right foot**), Reverse Square, Backward Passing Change (Natural to Reverse) and Reverse Turn.
After: Forward Change (**Left foot**), Reverse Square, Backward Passing Change (Reverse to Natural) and Reverse Turn.

Hesitation Change
Before: Forward Change (**Left foot**), Natural Square, Backward Passing Change (Reverse to Natural) and Natural Turn
After: Forward Change (**Left foot**), Reverse Square, Backward Passing Change (Reverse to Natural) and Reverse Turn.

Practice Choreography

Routine One
Preparatory Position: Start facing Line of Dance, weight on the **Right foot** in Close Hold. End facing Line of Dance.
Forward Change on the **left foot**. Forward Change on the **right foot**. Repeat the Forward Changes moving down the Line of Dance. When approaching a corner, curve the Change Steps around the corner to end facing the new Line of Dance. Continue dancing the Change Steps making a complete circle in an anti-clockwise direction around the room.

Routine Two
Preparatory Position: Start facing Line of Dance, weight on the **Right foot** in Close Hold. End facing Line of Dance.
Dance three Forward Changes into a Natural Square (no turn). Dance three Forward Changes into a Reverse Square (no turn).

Routine Three
Preparatory Position: Start facing Line of Dance, weight on the **Right foot** in Close Hold. End facing Line of Dance.
Dance three Forward Changes into a Natural Turn ($\frac{1}{2}$ turn to right, over steps

1-6). Repeat the Natural Turn (½ to right, over steps 1-6), to end facing Line of Dance.

Dance three Forward Changes into a Reverse Turn (½ turn to left, over steps 1-6). Repeat the Reverse Turn (½ to left, over steps 1-6), to end facing Line of Dance.

Routine Four

Preparatory Position: Start facing diagonally to Wall, weight on the **Right foot** in Close Hold. End facing diagonally to Wall.

Dance a Reverse Square. Backward Passing Change (Reverse to Natural). Dance a Natural Square. Backward Passing Change (Natural to Reverse).

Routine Five

Preparatory Position: Start facing diagonally to Wall, weight on the **Right foot** in Close Hold. End facing diagonally to Wall.

Forward Change (**Left foot**). Natural Turn. Forward Change (**Right foot**). Reverse Turn. Repeat this routine down the side of the room.

When approaching a corner, substitute the Natural Turn with the Hesitation Change. Start on the new side of the room with the Forward Change (**Left foot**).

Wondering what music to use? See page 143 for our recommendations!

Quick Waltz (Viennese Waltz)

Time signature: ¾; three beats to the bar.

Rhythm: Each step occupies one beat of music.

Tempo: Approximately 60 bars per minute. (240 mm.)

The name 'Quick Waltz' is given to the social version of the Viennese Waltz. The Quick Waltz is often played at social dance functions at a tempo ranging from 40 bars per minute (160 mm.) to the recommended tempo of 60 bars per minute (240 mm.).

Action

Over each set of three counts use a rise and falling action – down on 1, up on 2, up on 3. At the end of three, lower the supporting foot and at the same time take the following step to the side on the count of one.

New Terms

Brush: When the foot is moved from an open position to a closed position without weight.

Pendulum Step to the Right

Man's steps

Preparatory Position: Start facing Line of Dance, weight on **left foot**, in Close Hold. End facing Line of Dance.

Step	Foot Position and Direction	Turn	Footwork	Body Alignment
1.	**Right foot** to the side, allowing the **left foot** to brush towards **right foot**. Hold the body weight on the **right foot**.	Nil.	Ball flat ball (**right foot**) ball (**left foot.**)	Facing Line of Dance.

Rhythm: 1 – 2 – 3
Calling Cues: Side – Brush – Hold

Lady's steps

Preparatory Position: Start backing Line of Dance, weight on **right foot**, in Close Hold. End backing Line of Dance.

Step	Foot Position and Direction	Turn	Footwork	Body Alignment
1.	**Left foot** to the side, allowing **right foot** to brush towards **left foot**. Hold the body weight on the **left foot**.	Nil.	Ball flat ball (**left foot**) ball(**right foot.**)	Backing Line of Dance.

Rhythm: 1 – 2 – 3
Calling Cues: Side – Brush – Hold

Pendulum Step to the Left

Man's steps

Preparatory Position: Start facing Line of Dance, weight on **right foot**, in Close Hold. End facing Line of Dance.

Step	Foot Position and Direction	Turn	Footwork	Body Alignment
1.	**Left foot** to the side, allowing **right foot** to brush towards **left foot**. Hold the body weight on the **left foot**.	Nil.	Ball flat ball (**left foot**)ball (**right foot.**)	Facing Line of Dance.

Rhythm: 1 – 2 – 3
Calling Cues: Side – Brush – Hold

Lady's steps

Preparatory Position: Start backing Line of Dance, weight on **left foot**, in Close Hold. End backing Line of Dance.

Step	Foot Position and Direction	Turn	Footwork	Body Alignment
1.	**Right foot** to the side, allowing **left foot** to brush towards **right foot**. Hold the body weight on the **right foot**.	Nil	Ball flat ball (**right foot**) ball (**left foot.**)	Backing Line of Dance.

Rhythm: 1 – 2 – 3
Calling Cues: Side – Brush – Hold

Forward Change (Left foot)

Man's steps

Normally used after a Reverse Turn to a Natural Turn.
Preparatory Position: Start facing diagonally to Wall, weight on the **right foot**, in Close Hold. End facing diagonally to Wall.

Step	Foot Position and Direction	Turn	Footwork	Body Alignment
1.	**Left foot** forward, diagonally to Wall.	Nil.	Heel flat.	Facing diagonally to Wall.
2.	**Right foot** to side, moving diagonally to Wall against Line of Dance.	Nil.	Ball.	Facing diagonally to Wall.
3.	Close **left foot** to **right foot**.	Nil.	Ball flat.	Facing diagonally to Wall.

Rhythm: 1 – 2 – 3
Calling Cues: Forward – Side – Close

Lady's steps

Preparatory Position: Start backing diagonally to Wall, weight on the **left foot**, in Close Hold. End backing diagonally to Wall.

Step	Foot Position and Direction	Turn	Footwork	Body Alignment
1.	**Right foot** back, diagonally to Wall.	Nil.	Ball flat.	Backing diagonally to Wall.
2.	**Left foot** to side, moving diagonally to Wall against Line of Dance.	Nil.	Ball.	Backing diagonally to Wall.
3.	Close **right foot** to **left foot**.	Nil.	Ball flat.	Backing diagonally to Wall.

Rhythm: 1 – 2 – 3
Calling Cues: Back – Side – Close

Forward Change (Right foot)

Man's steps

Normally used from a Natural Turn to a Reverse Turn.
Preparatory Position: Start facing diagonally to Centre, weight on the **left foot**, in Close Hold. End facing diagonally to Centre.

Step	Foot Position and Direction	Turn	Footwork	Body Alignment
1.	**Right foot** forward, diagonally to Centre.	Nil.	Heel flat.	Facing diagonally to Centre.
2.	**Left foot** to side, moving diagonally to Centre against Line of Dance.	Nil.	Ball.	Facing diagonally to Centre.
3.	Close **right foot** to **left foot**.	Nil.	Ball flat.	Facing diagonally to Centre.

Rhythm: 1 – 2 – 3
Calling Cues: Forward – Side – Close

Lady's steps

Preparatory Position: Start backing diagonally to Centre, weight on the **right foot**, in Close Hold. End backing diagonally to Centre.

Step	Foot Position and Direction	Turn	Footwork	Body Alignment
1.	**Left foot** back, diagonally to Centre.	Nil.	Ball flat.	Backing diagonally to Centre.
2.	**Right foot** to side, diagonally to Centre against Line of Dance.	Nil.	Ball.	Backing diagonally to Centre.
3.	Close **left foot** to **right foot**.	Nil.	Ball flat.	Backing diagonally to Centre.

Rhythm: 1 – 2 – 3
Calling Cues: Back – Side – Close

Right Turn (known also as the Natural Turn)

Man's steps

Preparatory Position: Start facing diagonally to Wall, weight on the **left foot**, in Close Hold. End facing diagonally to Centre.

Step	Foot Position and Direction	Turn	Footwork	Body Alignment
1.	**Right foot** forward, diagonally to Wall, between partner's feet.	Body turn to right.	Heel flat.	Facing diagonally to Wall.
2.	**Left foot** to the side, diagonally to Wall.	Continue to turn.	Ball.	Backing diagonally to Centre.
3.	Close **right foot** to **left foot**.	$\frac{3}{8}$ to right, over steps 1-3.	Ball flat.	Backing Line of Dance.
4.	**Left foot** to the side and slightly back, diagonally to Wall.	Body turn to right.	Ball flat.	Backing Line of Dance.
5.	**Right foot** to the side, along Line of Dance.	Continue to turn.	Ball.	Foot pointing diagonally to Centre.
6.	Close **left foot** to **right foot**.	$\frac{3}{8}$ to right, over steps 4-6.	Ball flat.	Facing diagonally to Centre.

Rhythm: 1 – 2 – 3 – 1 – 2 – 3
Calling Cues: Forward – Turn – Close – Back – Turn – Close

Lady's steps

Preparatory Position: Start backing diagonally to Wall, weight on **right foot**, in Close Hold. End backing diagonally to Centre.

Step	Foot Position and Direction	Turn	Footwork	Body Alignment
1.	**Left foot** to the side and slightly back, to Wall.	Body turn to right.	Ball flat.	Backing diagonally to Wall.
2.	**Right foot** to the side, diagonally to Wall.	Continue to turn.	Ball.	Foot pointing to Line of Dance.

Step	Foot Position and Direction	Turn	Footwork	Body Alignment
3.	Close **left foot** to **right foot**.	⅜ to right, over steps 1-3.	Ball flat.	Facing Line of Dance.
4.	**Right foot** forward, down Line of Dance, between partner's feet.	Body turn to right.	Heel flat.	Facing Line of Dance.
5.	**Left foot** to the side, along Line of Dance.	Continue to turn.	Ball.	Backing Centre.
6.	Close **right foot** to **left foot**.	⅜ to right, over steps 4-6.	Ball flat.	Backing diagonally to Centre.

Rhythm: 1 – 2 – 3 – 1 – 2 – 3
Calling Cues: Back – Turn – Close – Forward – Turn – Close

Left Turn (known also as the Reverse Turn)

Man's steps

Preparatory Position: Start facing diagonally to Centre, weight on **right foot**, in Close Hold. End facing diagonally to Wall.

Step	Foot Position and Direction	Turn	Footwork	Body Alignment
1.	**Left foot** forward, diagonally to Centre.	Body turn to left.	Heel flat.	Facing diagonally to Centre.
2.	**Right foot** to the side, diagonally to Centre.	Continue to turn.	Ball.	Backing diagonally to Wall.
3.	Close **left foot** to **right foot**.	⅜ to left, over steps 1-3.	Ball flat.	Backing Line of Dance.
4.	**Right foot** to side and slightly back, down Line of Dance.	Body turn to left.	Ball flat.	Backing Line of Dance.
5.	**Left foot** to the side, along Line of Dance.	Continue to turn.	Ball.	Foot pointing diagonally to Wall.
6.	Close **right foot** to **left foot**.	⅜ to left, over steps 4-6.	Ball flat.	Facing diagonally to Wall.

Rhythm: 1 – 2 – 3 – 1 – 2 – 3
Calling Cues: Forward – Turn – Close – Back – Turn – Close

Lady's steps

Preparatory Position: Start backing diagonally Centre, weight on **left foot**, in Close Hold. End backing diagonally to Wall.

Step	Foot Position and Direction	Turn	Footwork	Body Alignment
1.	**Right foot** to side and slightly back, to Centre.	Body turn to left.	Ball flat.	Backing diagonally to Centre.
2.	**Left foot** to the side, diagonally to Centre.	Continue to turn.	Ball.	Foot pointing to Line of Dance.
3.	Close **right foot** to **left foot**.	⅜ to left, over steps 1-3.	Ball flat.	Facing Line of Dance.
4.	**Left foot** forward, down Line of Dance, between partner's feet.	Body turn to left.	Heel flat.	Facing Line of Dance.
5.	**Right foot** to the side, along Line of Dance.	Continue to turn.	Ball.	Backing Wall.
6.	Close **left foot** to **right foot**.	⅜ to left, over steps 4-6.	Ball flat.	Backing diagonally to Wall.

Rhythm: 1 – 2 – 3 – 1 – 2 – 3
Calling Cues: Back – Turn – Close – Forward – Turn – Close

Precedes and Follows

Pendulum Step to Right
Before: Pendulum Step to the Left, Forward Change (**Left foot**) and Right Turn.
After: Pendulum Step to the Left, Forward Change (**Left foot**) and Left Turn.

Pendulum Step to Left
Before: Pendulum Step to the Right, Forward Change (**Right foot**) and Left Turn.
After: Pendulum Step to the Right, Forward Change (**Right foot**) and Right Turn.

Forward Change (Left foot)
Before: Pendulum Step to the Right, Forward Change (**Right foot**) and Left Turn.
After: Pendulum Step to the Right, Forward Change (**Right foot**) and Right Turn.

Forward Change (Right foot)

Before: Pendulum Step to the Left, Forward Change (**Left foot**) and Right Turn.
After: Pendulum Step to the Left, Forward Change (**Left foot**) and Left Turn.

Right Turn

Before: Pendulum Step to the Left, Forward Change (**Left foot**) and Right Turn.
After: Pendulum Step to the Right, Forward Change (**Right foot**) and Right Turn.

Left Turn

Before: Pendulum Step to the Right, Forward Change (**Right foot**) and Left Turn.
After: Pendulum Step to the Left, Forward Change (**Left foot**) and Left Turn.

Practice Choreography

Routine One

Preparatory Position: Start facing Line of Dance, weight on the **left foot** in Close Hold. End facing Line of Dance.
Pendulum Step on the Right Foot. Pendulum Step on the Left Foot. Pendulum Step on the Right Foot. Pendulum Step on the Left Foot.

Routine Two

Preparatory Position: Start facing diagonally to Wall, weight on the **left foot** in Close Hold. End facing diagonally to Wall.
Right Turn (½). Right Turn (½).

Routine Three

Preparatory Position: Start facing diagonally to Wall, weight on the **left foot** in Close Hold. End facing diagonally to Wall.
Pendulum Step on the Right Foot. Pendulum Step on the Left Foot. Right Turn (½). Right Turn (½).

Routine Four

Preparatory Position: Start facing diagonally to Centre, weight on the **Right foot** in Close Hold. End facing diagonally to Centre.
Pendulum Step on the Left Foot. Pendulum Step on the Right Foot. Left Turn (½). Left Turn (½).

Routine Five

Preparatory Position: Start facing diagonally to Wall, weight on the **left foot** in Close Hold. End facing diagonally to Wall.
Pendulum Step on the Right Foot. Pendulum Step on the Left Foot. Right Turn. Forward Change (**Right foot**). Left Turn. Forward Change (**Left foot**).

Social Foxtrot (Slow Rhythm)

Time signature: 4/4; four beats to the bar.

Rhythm: Slow = 2 beats. Quick = 1 beat.

Tempo: Wide range from 20 to 30 bars per minute. (80–120mm.)

It is worth spending time mastering the figures for the foxtrot as many can be used in the quickstep – an easy way of doubling your repertoire of dances. The social foxtrot is much less difficult to learn than the slow foxtrot, and you will be able to dance it to the full range of music written in 4/4 time.

Walks

The walk action of the Foxtrot has the same foot action as the Waltz.

Footwork

All steps timed Quick preceding a closing step with a weight change use the footwork of Ball. However, it is correct to lower to the flat of the foot when the tempo is very slow.

Action

Each step is taken with a slight sway. On **Left foot forward**, or backward, sway slightly to the left. **Right foot forward**, or backward, is accompanied by a slight sway to the right. The sway is not so pronounced on the steps timed Quick.

Quarter Turn to Right

Man's steps

Preparatory Position: Start facing diagonally to Wall, weight on the **right foot**, in Close Hold. End backing diagonally to Centre.

Step	Foot Position and Direction	Turn	Footwork	Body Alignment
1.	**Left foot** forward, diagonally to Wall.	Nil.	Heel flat.	Facing diagonally to Wall.
2.	**Right foot** forward, diagonally to Wall.	Body turn to right.	Heel flat.	Facing diagonally to Wall.
3.	**Left foot** to side, along Line of Dance.	Continue to turn.	Ball.	Backing Centre.
4.	Close **right foot** to **left foot**.	¼ to right, over steps 2-4.	Ball flat.	Backing diagonally to Centre.

Rhythm: Slow – Slow – Quick – Quick
Calling Cues: Forward – Forward – Turn – Close

Lady's steps

Preparatory Position: Start backing diagonally to Wall, weight on the **left foot**, in Close Hold. End facing diagonally to Centre.

Step	Foot Position and Direction	Turn	Footwork	Body Alignment
1.	**Right foot** back, diagonally to Wall.	Nil.	Ball flat.	Backing diagonally to Wall.
2.	**Left foot** back, diagonally to Wall.	Body turn to right.	Ball flat.	Backing diagonally to Wall.
3.	**Right foot** to side, along Line of Dance.	Continue to turn.	Ball.	Foot pointing diagonally to Centre.
4.	Close **left foot** to **right foot**.	¼ to right, over steps 2-4.	Ball flat.	Facing diagonally to Centre.

Rhythm: Slow – Slow – Quick – Quick
Calling Cues: Back – Back – Turn – Close

Quarter Turn to Left

Man's steps

Preparatory Position: Start backing diagonally to Centre, weight on the **right foot**, in Close Hold. End facing diagonally to Wall.

Step	Foot Position and Direction	Turn	Footwork	Body Alignment
1.	**Left foot** back, diagonally to Centre.	Nil.	Ball flat.	Backing diagonally to Centre.
2.	**Right foot** back, diagonally to Centre.	Body turn to left.	Ball flat.	Backing diagonally to Centre.
3.	**Left foot** to side, along Line of Dance.	Continue to turn.	Ball.	Foot pointing diagonally to Wall.
4.	Close **right foot** to **left foot**.	¼ to left, over steps 2-4.	Ball flat.	Facing diagonally to Wall.

Rhythm: Slow – Slow – Quick – Quick
Calling Cues: Back – Back – Turn – Close

Lady's steps

Preparatory Position: Start facing diagonally to Centre, weight on the **left foot**, in Close Hold. End backing diagonally to Wall.

Step	Foot Position and Direction	Turn	Footwork	Body Alignment
1.	**Right foot** forward, diagonally to Centre.	Nil.	Heel flat.	Facing diagonally to Centre.
2.	**Left foot** forward, diagonally to Centre.	Body turn to left.	Heel flat.	Facing diagonally to Centre.
3.	**Right foot** to side, along Line of Dance.	Continue to turn.	Ball.	Backing Wall.
4.	Close **left foot** to **right foot**.	$\frac{1}{4}$ to left, over steps 2-4.	Ball flat.	Backing diagonally to Wall.

Rhythm: Slow – Slow – Quick – Quick
Calling Cues: Forward – Forward – Turn – Close

Natural Pivot Turn

Man's steps

Preparatory Position: Start facing diagonally to Wall, weight on the **right foot**, in Close Hold. End backing diagonally to Centre against Line of Dance.

Step	Foot Position and Direction	Turn	Footwork	Body Alignment
1.	**Left foot** forward, diagonally to Wall.	Nil.	Heel flat.	Facing diagonally to Wall.
2.	**Right foot** forward, diagonally to Wall.	Body turn to right.	Heel flat.	Facing diagonally to Wall.
3.	**Left foot** to side, diagonally to Wall.	Continue to turn.	Ball.	Backing diagonally to Centre.
4.	Close **right foot** to **left foot**.	$\frac{3}{8}$ to right, over steps 2-4.	Ball flat.	Backing Line of Dance.
5.	**Left foot** to side and slightly back, down Line of Dance.	Body turn to right.	Ball flat.	Backing Line of Dance.
6.	**Right foot** forward, to Centre.	Continue to turn.	Heel flat.	Facing Centre.

| 7. | **Left foot** to side, to Centre. | Continue to turn. | Ball. | Backing against Line of Dance. |
| 8. | Close **right foot** to **left foot**. | ⅜ to right, over steps 5-8. | Ball flat. | Backing diagonally to Centre against Line of Dance. |

Rhythm: Slow – Slow – Quick – Quick – Slow – Slow – Quick – Quick
Calling Cues: Forward – Forward – Turn – Close – Back – Spin – Spin – Close

Lady's steps

Preparatory Position: Start backing diagonally to Wall, weight on the **left foot** in Close Hold. End facing diagonally to Centre against Line of Dance.

Step	Foot Position and Direction	Turn	Footwork	Body Alignment
1.	**Right foot** back, diagonally to Wall.	Nil.	Ball flat.	Backing diagonally to Wall.
2.	**Left foot** back, diagonally to Wall.	Body turn to right.	Ball flat.	Backing diagonally to Wall.
3.	**Right foot** to side, diagonally to Wall.	Continue to turn.	Ball.	Foot pointing to Line of Dance.
4.	Close **left foot** to **right foot**.	⅜ to right, over steps 2-4.	Ball flat.	Facing Line of Dance.
5.	**Right foot** forward between partner's feet, down Line of Dance.	Body turn to right.	Heel flat.	Facing Line of Dance.
6.	**Left foot** to side, along Line of Dance.	Continue to turn.	Ball.	Backing Centre.
7.	**Right foot** to side, to Centre.	Continue to turn.	Ball.	Foot pointing diagonally to Centre against Line of Dance.
8.	Close **left foot** to **right foot**.	⅜ to right, over steps 5-8.	Ball flat.	Facing diagonally to Centre against Line of Dance.

Rhythm: Slow – Slow – Quick – Quick – Slow – Slow – Quick – Quick
Calling Cues: Back – Back – Turn – Close – Forward – Spin – Spin – Close

Natural Rocking Turn

Man's steps

Preparatory Position: Start facing diagonally to Wall, weight on the **right foot**, in Close Hold. End backing diagonally to Centre against Line of Dance.

Step	Foot Position and Direction	Turn	Footwork	Body Alignment
1.	**Left foot** forward, diagonally to Wall.	Nil.	Heel flat.	Facing diagonally to Wall.
2.	**Right foot** forward, diagonally to Wall.	Body turn to right.	Heel flat.	Facing diagonally to Wall.
3.	**Left foot** to side, diagonally to Wall.	Continue to turn.	Ball.	Backing diagonally to Centre.
4.	Close **right foot** to **left foot**.	⅜ to right, over steps 2-4.	Ball flat.	Backing Line of Dance.
5.	**Left foot** to side and slightly back, down Line of Dance.	Body turn to right.	Ball flat.	Backing Line of Dance.
6.	**Right foot** forward, diagonally to Centre against Line of Dance.	Continue to turn.	Heel flat.	Facing diagonally to Centre against Line of Dance.
7.	Replace weight back to **left foot**, to Wall.	Continue to turn.	Ball flat.	Backing Wall.
8.	Replace weight forward to **right foot**, diagonally to Centre.	Continue to turn.	Heel flat.	Facing diagonally to Centre.
9.	**Left foot** to side, to Centre.	Continue to turn.	Ball.	Backing Line of Dance.
10.	Close **right foot** to **left foot**.	⅜ to right, over steps 5-10.	Ball flat.	Backing diagonally to Centre against Line of Dance.

Rhythm: Slow – Slow – Quick – Quick – Slow – Slow – Slow – Slow – Quick – Quick

Calling Cues: Forward – Forward – Turn – Close – Back – Rock – Rock – Rock – Side – Close

Lady's steps

Preparatory Position: Start backing diagonally to Wall, weight on the **left foot** in Close Hold. End facing diagonally to Centre against Line of Dance.

Step	Foot Position and Direction	Turn	Footwork	Body Alignment
1.	**Right foot** back, diagonally to Wall.	Nil.	Ball flat.	Backing diagonally to Wall.
2.	**Left foot** back, diagonally to Wall.	Body turn to right.	Ball flat.	Backing diagonally to Wall.
3.	**Right foot** to side, diagonally to Wall.	Continue to turn.	Ball.	Foot pointing to Line of Dance.
4.	Close **left foot** to **right foot**.	⅜ to right, over steps 2-4.	Ball flat.	Facing Line of Dance.
5.	**Right foot** forward between partner's feet, down Line of Dance.	Body turn to right.	Heel flat.	Facing Line of Dance.
6.	**Left foot** back, diagonally to Centre against Line of Dance.	Continue to turn.	Ball flat.	Backing diagonally to Centre against Line of Dance.
7.	Replace weight forward to **right foot**, to Wall.	Continue to turn.	Heel flat.	Facing Wall.
8.	Replace weight back to **left foot**, diagonally to Centre.	Continue to turn.	Ball flat.	Backing diagonally to Centre.
9.	**Right foot** to side, to Centre.	Continue to turn.	Ball.	Foot pointing diagonally to Centre against Line of Dance.
10.	Close **left foot** to **right foot**.	⅝ to right, over steps 5-10.	Ball flat.	Facing diagonally to Centre against Line of Dance.

Rhythm: Slow – Slow – Quick – Quick – Slow – Slow – Slow – Slow – Quick – Quick
Calling Cues: Back – Back – Turn – Close – Forward – Rock – Rock – Rock – Side – Close

Left Pivot Turn

Man's steps

Preparatory Position: Start facing diagonally to Centre, weight on the **right foot**, in Close Hold. End facing diagonally to Wall.

Step	Foot Position and Direction	Turn	Footwork	Body Alignment
1.	**Left foot** forward, diagonally to Centre.	Body turn to left.	Heel flat.	Facing diagonally to Centre.
2.	**Right foot** back, diagonally to Wall.	Continue to turn.	Ball flat.	Backing diagonally to Wall.
3.	**Left foot** to side, to Wall.	Continue to turn.	Ball.	Foot pointing diagonally to Wall against Line of Dance.
4.	Close **right foot** to **left foot**.	½ to left, over steps 1-4.	Ball flat.	Facing diagonally to Wall against Line of Dance.
5.	**Left foot** forward, diagonally to Wall against Line of Dance.	Body turn to left.	Heel flat.	Facing diagonally to Wall against Line of Dance.
6.	**Right foot** back, to Centre.	Continue to turn.	Ball flat.	Backing Centre.
7.	**Left foot** to side, diagonally to Centre.	Continue to turn.	Ball.	Foot pointing diagonally to Wall.
8.	Close **right foot** to **left foot**.	¼ to left, over steps 5-8.	Ball flat.	Facing diagonally to Wall.

Rhythm: Slow – Slow – Quick – Quick – Slow – Slow – Quick – Quick
Calling Cues: Check – Back – Turn – Close – Check – Back – Turn – Close

Lady's steps

Preparatory Position: Start backing diagonally to Centre, weight on the **left foot**, in Close Hold. End backing diagonally to Wall.

Step	Foot Position and Direction	Turn	Footwork	Body Alignment
1.	**Right foot** back, diagonally to Centre.	Body turn to left.	Ball flat.	Backing diagonally to Centre.
2.	**Left foot** forward, diagonally to Wall.	Continue to turn.	Heel flat.	Facing diagonally to Wall.

3.	**Right foot** to side, to Wall.	Continue to turn.	Ball.	Backing Line of Dance.
4.	Close **left foot** to **right foot**.	½ to left, over steps 1-4.	Ball flat.	Backing diagonally to Wall against Line of Dance.
5.	**Right foot** back, diagonally to Wall against Line of Dance.	Body turn to left.	Ball flat.	Backing diagonally to Wall against Line of Dance.
6.	**Left foot** forward, to Centre.	Continue to turn.	Heel flat.	Facing Centre.
7.	**Right foot** to side, diagonally to Centre.	Continue to turn.	Ball.	Backing Wall.
8.	Close **left foot** to **right foot**.	¼ to left, over steps 5-8.	Ball flat.	Backing diagonally to Wall.

Rhythm: Slow – Slow – Quick – Quick – Slow – Slow – Quick – Quick
Calling Cues: Check – Forward – Turn – Close – Check – Forward – Turn – Close

Conversation Piece

Man's steps

Preparatory Position: Start facing diagonally to Wall, weight on the **right foot**, in Close Hold. End facing diagonally to Wall.

Step	Foot Position and Direction	Turn	Footwork	Body Alignment
1.	**Left foot** forward, diagonally to Wall.	No turn over steps 1-8.	Heel flat.	Facing diagonally to Wall.
2.	**Right foot** forward, diagonally to Wall.		Heel flat.	Facing diagonally to Wall.
3.	**Left foot** to side in Promenade position, along Line of Dance.		Ball.	Facing diagonally to Wall.
4.	Close **right foot** to **left foot**.		Ball flat.	Facing diagonally to Wall.
5.	**Left foot** to side in Promenade position, along Line of Dance.		Heel flat.	Facing diagonally to Wall.
6.	**Right foot** forward and across **left foot** in Promenade position.		Heel flat.	Facing diagonally to Wall.

7.	Left foot to side in Promenade position, along Line of Dance.		Ball	Facing diagonally to Wall.
8.	Close **right foot** to **left foot** in Promenade position.		Ball flat.	Facing diagonally to Wall.
9.	**Left foot** to side, in Promenade position, along Line of Dance.	Nil.	Heel flat.	Facing diagonally to Wall.
10.	**Right foot** forward and across **left foot** in Promenade position.	Body turn to right.	Heel flat.	Facing diagonally to Wall.
11.	**Left foot** to side, along Line of Dance.	Continue to turn.	Ball.	Backing Centre.
12.	Close **right foot** to **left foot**.	¼ to right, over steps 10-12.	Ball flat.	Backing diagonally to Centre.
13.	**Left foot** back, diagonally to Centre.	Nil.	Ball flat.	Backing diagonally to Centre.
14.	**Right foot** back, diagonally to Centre.	Body turn to left.	Ball flat.	Backing diagonally to Centre.
15.	**Left foot** to side, along Line of Dance.	Continue to turn.	Ball.	Foot pointing diagonally to Wall.
16.	Close **right foot** to **left foot**.	¼ to left, over steps 14-16.	Ball flat.	Facing diagonally to Wall.

Rhythm: Slow – Slow – Quick – Quick – Slow – Slow – Quick – Quick – Slow – Slow – Quick – Quick – Slow – Slow – Quick – Quick
Calling Cues: Forward – Forward – Side – Close- Side – Forward – Side – Close – Side – Forward – Turn – Close – Back – Back – Turn – Close

Lady's steps

Preparatory Position: Start backing diagonally to Wall, weight on the **left foot** in Close Hold. End backing diagonally to Wall.

Step	Foot Position and Direction	Turn	Footwork	Body Alignment
1.	**Right foot** back, diagonally to Wall.	Nil.	Ball flat.	Backing diagonally to Wall.
2.	**Left foot** back, diagonally to Wall.	Nil.	Ball flat.	Backing diagonally to Wall.

3.	**Right foot** to side in Promenade position, along Line of Dance.	¼ to right.	Ball.	Facing diagonally to Centre.
4.	Close **left foot** to **right foot.**	Nil.	Ball flat.	Facing diagonally to Centre.
5.	**Right foot** to side in Promenade position, along Line of Dance.	Nil.	Heel flat.	Facing diagonally to Centre.
6.	**Left foot** forward and across **right foot** in Promenade position.	Nil.	Heel flat.	Facing diagonally to Centre.
7.	**Right foot** to side in Promenade position.	Nil.	Ball.	Facing diagonally to Centre.
8.	Close **left foot** to **right foot** in Promenade position.	Nil.	Ball flat.	Facing diagonally to Centre.
9.	**Right foot** to side in Promenade position, along Line of Dance.	Nil.	Heel flat.	Facing diagonally to Centre.
10.	**Left foot** forward and across **right foot** in Promenade position.	Nil.	Heel flat.	Facing diagonally to Centre.
11.	**Right foot** to side, along Line of Dance.	Nil.	Ball.	Facing diagonally to Centre.
12.	Close **left foot** to **right foot.**	Nil.	Ball flat.	Facing diagonally to Centre.
13.	**Right foot** forward, diagonally to Centre.	Nil.	Heel flat.	Facing diagonally to Centre.
14.	**Left foot** forward, diagonally to Centre.	Body turn to left.	Heel flat.	Facing diagonally to Centre.
15.	**Right foot** to side, along Line of Dance.	Continue to turn.	Ball.	Backing Wall.
16.	Close **left foot** to **right foot.**	¼ to left, over steps 14-16.	Ball flat.	Backing diagonally to Wall.

Rhythm: Slow – Slow – Quick – Quick – Slow – Slow – Quick – Quick – Slow – Slow – Quick – Quick – Slow – Slow – Quick – Quick
Calling Cues: Back – Back – Turn – Close – Side – Forward – Side – Close – Side – Forward – Side – Close – Forward – Forward – Turn – Close

Rhythm Break (also known as the Side Step)

Man's steps

Preparatory Position: Start facing diagonally to Wall, weight on the **right foot**, in Close Hold. End facing diagonally to Wall.

Step	Foot Position and Direction	Turn	Footwork	Body Alignment
1.	**Left foot** to side, diagonally to Centre.	Nil.	Ball flat.	Facing diagonally to Wall.
2.	Close **right foot** to **left foot**, without weight.	Nil.	Ball.	Facing diagonally to Wall.
3.	**Right foot** to side, diagonally to Wall against Line of Dance.	Nil.	Ball flat.	Facing diagonally to Wall.
4.	Close **left foot** to **right foot**, without weight.	Nil.	Ball.	Facing diagonally to Wall.
5.	**Left foot** to side, diagonally to Centre.	Nil.	Ball flat.	Facing diagonally to Wall.
6.	Close **right foot** to **left foot**.	Nil.	Ball flat.	Facing diagonally to Wall.

Rhythm: Quick – Quick – Quick – Quick – Quick – Quick
Calling Cues: Side – Tap – Side – Tap – Side – Close

Lady's steps

Preparatory Position: Start backing diagonally to Wall, weight on the **left foot** in Close Hold. End backing diagonally to Wall.

Step	Foot Position and Direction	Turn	Footwork	Body Alignment
1.	**Right foot** to side, diagonally to Centre.	Nil.	Ball flat.	Backing diagonally to Wall.
2.	Close **left foot** to **right foot**, without weight.	Nil.	Ball.	Backing diagonally to Wall.
3.	**Left foot** to side, diagonally to Wall against Line of Dance.	Nil.	Ball flat.	Backing diagonally to Wall.

4.	Close **right foot** to **left foot**, without weight.	Nil.	Ball.	Backing diagonally to Wall.
5.	**Right foot** to side, diagonally to Centre.	Nil.	Ball flat.	Backing diagonally to Wall.
6.	Close **left foot** to **right foot**.	Nil.	Ball flat.	Backing diagonally to Wall.

Rhythm: Quick – Quick – Quick – Quick – Quick – Quick
Calling Cues: Side – Tap – Side – Tap – Side – Close

Precedes and Follows

Quarter Turn to Right
Before: Quarter Turn to Left, Rhythm Break, Conversation Piece and Left Pivot Turn.
After: Quarter Turn to Left and Rhythm Break.

Quarter Turn to Left
Before: Quarter Turn to Right, Rhythm Break, Conversation Piece, Natural Rocking Turn and Natural Pivot Turn.
After: Quarter Turn to Right, Rhythm Break, Conversation Piece, Natural Rocking Turn and Natural Pivot Turn.

Natural Pivot Turn
Before: Quarter Turn to Left, Rhythm Break, Conversation Piece and Left Pivot Turn.
After: Quarter Turn to Left and Rhythm Break.

Natural Rocking Turn
Before: Quarter Turn to Left, Rhythm Break, Conversation Piece and Left Pivot Turn.
After: Quarter Turn to Left and Rhythm Break.

Left Pivot Turn
Before: Quarter Turn to Left and Rhythm Break.
After: Quarter Turn to Right, Rhythm Break, Conversation Piece, Natural Rocking Turn and Natural Pivot Turn.

Conversation Piece
Before: Quarter Turn to Left, Rhythm Break, Conversation Piece and Left Pivot Turn.
After: Quarter Turn to Right, Rhythm Break, Conversation Piece, Natural Rocking Turn and Natural Pivot Turn.

Rhythm Break

Before: Quarter Turn to Right, Quarter Turn to Left, Rhythm Break, Conversation Piece, Natural Rocking Turn and Natural Pivot Turn.

After: Quarter Turn to Right, Rhythm Break, Conversation Piece, Natural Rocking Turn and Natural Pivot Turn.

Practice Choreography

Routine One

Preparatory Position: Start facing diagonally to Wall, weight on the **right foot**, in Close Hold. End facing diagonally to Wall.

Quarter Turn to Right. Quarter Turn to Left. Repeat moving around the room in an anti-clockwise direction.

Routine Two

Preparatory Position: Start facing diagonally to Wall, weight on the **right foot**, in Close Hold. End facing diagonally to Wall.

Quarter Turn to Right. Quarter Turn to Left. Conversation Piece. Repeat all.

Routine Three

Preparatory Position: Start facing diagonally to Wall, weight on the **right foot**, in Close Hold. End facing diagonally to Wall.

Quarter Turn to Right. Quarter Turn to Left. Rhythm Break. Natural Rocking Turn. Quarter Turn to Left. (End facing diagonally to Centre.) Left Pivot Turn.

Routine Four

Preparatory Position: Start facing diagonally to Wall, weight on the **right foot**, in Close Hold. End facing diagonally to Wall.

Quarter Turn to Right. Rhythm Break. Quarter Turn to Left. Rhythm Break. Natural Rocking Turn. Quarter Turn to Left. (End facing diagonally to Centre.) Left Pivot Turn.

Routine Five

Preparatory Position: Start facing diagonally to Wall, weight on the **right foot**, in Close Hold. End facing diagonally to Wall.

Dance 1 to 8 of the Conversation Piece. Dance Rhythm Break in Promenade position. Dance 9 to 16 Conversation Piece. Natural Pivot Turn. Quarter Turn to Left. (End facing diagonally to Centre.) Double Rhythm Break (12 counts) Left Pivot Turn. Natural Rocking Turn. Quarter Turn to Left (Start backing diagonally to Centre against Line of Dance, making no turn to end facing diagonally to Wall.)

Social Foxtrot (Quick Rhythm)

Time signature: 4/4; four beats to the bar.

Rhythm: *Slow = 2 beats, Quick = 1 beat.*

Tempo: Approximately 50 bars per minute. (200mm.)

This is a fast, flowing dance which is really enjoyable once you have mastered the footwork. As you have practised some of the figures at a more sedate pace in the social foxtrot, you will soon be cutting a dash. The dance fits a remarkable range of modern music – in fact, almost anything with a strong 4/4 rhythm. All the figures used in the foxtrot can be used, plus the following new figures.

Footwork

All steps timed Quick which precede a closing step with a weight change use the footwork of Ball.

Action

Each step is taken with a slight sway. On 'Left foot forward', or backward, make a slight sway to the left. Similarly, '**Right foot** forward', or backward, indicates a slight sway to the right. The sway is less pronounced on the steps timed Quick.

Cross Chassé to Back Corté

Man's steps

Preparatory Position: Start facing diagonally to Wall, weight on the **right foot**, in Close Hold. End facing diagonally to Wall.

Step	Foot Position and Direction	Turn	Footwork	Body Alignment
1.	**Left foot** forward, diagonally to Wall.	Nil.	Heel flat.	Facing diagonally to Wall.
2.	**Right foot** to side, a short step, diagonally to Wall against Line of Dance.	Nil.	Ball.	Facing diagonally to Wall.
3.	Close **left foot** to **right foot**.	Nil.	Ball flat.	Facing diagonally to Wall.
4.	**Right foot** forward, outside partner and Check, diagonally to Wall.	Nil.	Heel flat.	Facing diagonally to Wall.
5.	Transfer weight back to **left foot**, diagonally to Centre against Line of Dance.	Nil.	Ball flat.	Backing diagonally to Centre against Line of Dance.

6.	**Right foot** to side, a short step, diagonally to Wall against Line of Dance, partner in line.	Nil.	Ball.	Facing diagonally to Wall.
7.	Close **left foot** to **right foot**.	Nil.	Ball flat.	Facing diagonally to Wall.

Rhythm: Slow – Quick – Quick – Slow – Slow – Quick – Quick
Calling Cues: Forward – Side – Close – Check – Back – Side – Close

Lady's steps

Preparatory Position: Start backing diagonally to Wall, weight on the **left foot**, in Close Hold. End backing diagonally to Wall.

Step	Foot Position and Direction	Turn	Footwork	Body Alignment
1.	**Right foot** back, diagonally to Wall.	Nil.	Ball flat.	Backing diagonally to Wall.
2.	**Left foot** to side, a short step, diagonally to Wall against Line of Dance.	Nil.	Ball.	Backing diagonally to Wall.
3.	Close **right foot** to **left foot**.	Nil.	Ball flat.	Backing diagonally to Wall.
4.	**Left foot** back and Check, diagonally to Wall, partner outside.	Nil.	Ball flat.	Backing diagonally to Wall.
5.	Transfer weight forward to **right foot**, diagonally to Centre against Line of Dance.	Nil.	Heel flat.	Facing diagonally to Centre against Line of Dance.
6.	**Left foot** to side, a short step, diagonally to Wall against Line of Dance, partner in line.	Nil.	Ball.	Backing diagonally to Wall.
7.	Close **right foot** to **left foot**.	Nil.	Ball flat.	Backing diagonally to Wall.

Rhythm: Slow – Quick – Quick – Slow – Slow – Quick – Quick
Calling Cues: Back – Side – Close – Check – Forward – Side – Close

Forward Lock Step

Steps for man and lady

Preparatory Position: Start facing diagonally to Wall, weight on the **left foot**, in Close Hold. End facing diagonally to Wall.

Step	Foot Position and Direction	Turn	Footwork	Body Alignment
1.	**Right foot** forward, diagonally to Wall, outside partner.	Nil.	Heel flat.	Facing diagonally to Wall.
2.	**Left foot** sideways, along Line of Dance.	Nil.	Ball.	Facing diagonally to Wall.
3.	Cross **right foot** behind **left foot**.	Nil.	Ball.	Facing diagonally to Wall.
4.	**Left foot** sideways, along Line of Dance.	Nil.	Ball flat.	Facing diagonally to Wall.
5.	**Right foot** forward, diagonally to Wall, outside partner.	Nil.	Heel flat.	Facing diagonally to Wall.

Rhythm: Slow – Quick – Quick – Slow – Slow
Calling Cues: Forward – Step – Cross – Step – Forward
Note: When the man dances the Forward Lock Step, the lady dances a Backward Lock Step. Step 1 can also be commenced in line with partner.

Backward Lock Step

Steps for man and lady

Preparatory Position: Start backing diagonally to Wall, weight on the **right foot**, in Close Hold. End backing diagonally to Wall.

Step	Foot Position and Direction	Turn	Footwork	Body Alignment
1.	**Left foot** back, diagonally to Wall, partner outside.	Nil.	Ball flat.	Backing diagonally to Wall.
2.	**Right foot** sideways, along Line of Dance.	Nil.	Ball.	Backing diagonally to Wall.
3.	Cross **left foot** in front of **right foot**.	Nil.	Ball.	Backing diagonally to Wall.

| 4. | **Right foot** sideways, along Line of Dance. | Nil. | Ball flat. | Backing diagonally to Wall. |
| 5. | **Left foot** back, diagonally to Wall, partner outside. | Nil. | Ball flat. | Backing diagonally to Wall. |

Rhythm: Slow – Quick – Quick – Slow – Slow
Calling Cues: Back – Step – Cross – Step – Back
Note: When the man dances the Backward Lock Step, the lady dances the Forward Lock Step.

Natural Spin Turn

Man's steps

Preparatory Position: Start facing diagonally to Wall, weight on the **left foot**, in Close Hold. End backing diagonally to Centre against Line of Dance.

Step	Foot Position and Direction	Turn	Footwork	Body Alignment
1.	**Right foot** forward, diagonally to Wall, between partner's feet.	Body turn to right.	Heel flat.	Facing diagonally to Wall.
2.	**Left foot** to the side, diagonally to Wall.	Continue to turn.	Ball.	Backing diagonally to Centre.
3.	Close **right foot** to **left foot**.	⅜ to right, over steps 1-3.	Ball flat.	Backing Line of Dance.
4.	**Left foot** to the side and slightly back, down Line of Dance.	Body turn to right.	Ball flat.	Backing Line of Dance.
5.	**Right foot** forward, diagonally to Centre.	Continue to turn.	Heel flat.	Facing diagonally to Centre.
6.	**Left foot** to side, to Centre.	⅜ to right, over steps 4-6.	Ball flat.	Backing diagonally to Centre against Line of Dance .

Rhythm: Slow – Quick – Quick – Slow – Slow – Slow
Calling Cues: Forward – Turn – Close – Spin – Spin – Spin

Natural Spin Turn

Lady's steps

Preparatory Position: Start backing diagonally to Wall, weight on the **right foot**, in Close Hold. End facing diagonally to Centre against Line of Dance.

Step	Foot Position and Direction	Turn	Footwork	Body Alignment
1.	**Left foot** to the side and slightly back, to Wall.	Body turn to right.	Ball flat.	Backing diagonally to Wall.
2.	**Right foot** to the side, diagonally to Wall.	Continue to turn.	Ball.	Foot pointing to Line of Dance.
3.	Close **left foot** to **right foot**.	⅜ to right, over steps 1-3.	Ball flat.	Facing Line of Dance.
4.	**Right foot** forward, down Line of Dance, between partner's feet.	Body turn to right.	Heel flat.	Facing Line of Dance.
5.	**Left foot** to the side, along Line of Dance.	Continue to turn.	Ball.	Backing Centre.
6.	Close **right foot** to **left foot**, without weight, then forward between partner's feet.	⅜ to right, over steps 4-6.	Ball flat.	Facing diagonally to Centre against Line of Dance.

Rhythm: Slow – Quick – Quick – Slow – Slow – Slow
Calling Cues: Back – Turn – Close – Spin – Spin – Spin

Progressive Chassé

Man's steps

Preparatory Position: Start backing diagonally to Centre, weight on the **left foot**, in Close Hold. End facing diagonally to Wall.

Step	Foot Position and Direction	Turn	Footwork	Body Alignment
1.	**Right foot** back, diagonally to Centre.	Body turn to left.	Ball flat.	Backing diagonally to Centre.

2.	**Left foot** to side, along Line of Dance.	Continue to turn.	Ball.	Foot pointing diagonally to Wall.
3.	Close **right foot** to **left foot**.	¼ to left, over steps 1-3.	Ball.	Facing diagonally to Wall.
4.	**Left foot** to side, along Line of Dance.	Nil.	Ball flat.	Facing diagonally to Wall.
5.	**Right foot** forward, diagonally to Wall, outside partner.	Nil.	Heel flat.	Facing diagonally to Wall.

Rhythm: Slow – Quick – Quick – Slow – Slow
Calling Cues: Back – Side – Close – Side – Forward

Lady's steps

Preparatory Position: Start facing diagonally to Centre, weight on the **right foot**, in Close Hold. End backing diagonally to Wall.

Step	Foot Position and Direction	Turn	Footwork	Body Alignment
1.	**Left foot** forward, diagonally to Centre.	Body turn to left.	Heel flat.	Facing diagonally to Centre.
2.	**Right foot** to side, along Line of Dance.	Continue to turn.	Ball.	Backing Wall.
3.	Close **left foot** to **right foot**.	¼ to left, over steps 1-3.	Ball.	Backing diagonally to Wall.
4.	**Right foot** to side, along Line of Dance.	Nil.	Ball flat.	Backing diagonally to Wall.
5.	**Left foot** back, diagonally to Wall, partner outside.	Nil.	Ball flat.	Backing diagonally to Wall.

Rhythm: Slow – Quick – Quick – Slow – Slow
Calling Cues: Forward – Side – Close – Side – Back

Precedes and Follows

Cross Chassé to Back Corté
Before: Quarter Turn to Left, Rhythm Break, Conversation Piece, Natural Rocking Turn and Natural Pivot Turn.
After: Forward Lock Step and Natural Spin Turn.

The Lock Steps
Before: Cross Chassé to Back Corté and Progressive Chassé.
After: Natural Spin Turn.

Natural Spin Turn
Before: Cross Chassé to Back Corté, Progressive Chassé and Forward Lock Step.
After: Progressive Chassé.

Practice Choreography
Routines one to five as for the Social Foxtrot, plus:

Routine Six
Preparatory Position: Start facing diagonally to Wall, weight on the **right foot**, in Close Hold. End facing diagonally to Wall.
Quarter Turn to Right. Quarter Turn to Left. Cross Chassé to Back Corté. Forward Lock Step. Natural Spin Turn. Progressive Chassé. Steps 4-7 Cross Chassé to Back Corté. (Step 7 Close with or without weight.)

You probably have some suitable music for practising these steps: see page 143 for some suggested tracks.

Tango

Time signature: 2/4, two beats to the bar; or 4/4, four beats to the bar.

Rhythm: *Slow = 1 beat. Quick = ½ beat.*

Tempo: 30 to 34 bars per minute. (2/4: 60 – 68mm. 4/4: 120 – 134mm.)

This is the European version of the Latin dance, but it remains more intense and sensual than most ballroom dances. The strong beat of the music most frequently chosen, straight body line and close hold make it a very intriguing dance to watch – but that's no excuse for not getting on the floor!

Tango Walk

The leg action of the walk differs considerably from the walks in the other dances. The main difference is that the body weight is delayed until the last moment before being transferred to the new supporting foot. As the normal forward Tango walk on the **right foot** is danced with a right side lead, there is always a tendency to curve the walk to the left. Although it is not incorrect to dance the Tango walk without the curve, the curve to the left should be encouraged in order to acquire the correct Tango character.

Closed Finish

When the man dances a Closed Finish, he deliberately places his feet into position. This action from the man causes the lady to complete her turn between two steps in feet and body. The lady's alignments are: 1. Facing diagonally to Centre, 2. Backing diagonally to Wall (Not Wall) and 3. Backing diagonally to Wall.

Tango Walks to Argentina Close

Man's steps

Preparatory Position: Start facing diagonally to Wall, weight on the **right foot**, in Close Hold. End facing diagonally to Wall.

Step	Foot Position and Direction	Turn	Footwork	Body Alignment
1.	**Left foot** forward, diagonally to Wall.	Nil.	Heel flat.	Facing diagonally to Wall.
2.	**Right foot** forward, diagonally to Wall.	Nil.	Heel flat.	Facing diagonally to Wall.

3.	**Left foot** forward, diagonally to Wall.	Nil.	Heel flat.	Facing diagonally to Wall.
4.	**Right foot** to side, a short step, diagonally to Wall against Line of Dance.	Nil.	Ball flat.	Facing diagonally to Wall.
5.	Tap **left foot** to **right foot**, without weight.	Nil.	Ball.	Facing diagonally to Wall.

Rhythm: Slow – Slow – Quick – Quick – Slow
Calling Cues: Forward – Forward – Step – Side – Tap
Note: A $\frac{1}{4}$ turn to the left can be made over steps 3 to 5.

Lady's steps

Preparatory Position: Start backing diagonally to Wall, weight on the **left foot**, in Close Hold. End backing diagonally to Wall.

Step	Foot Position and Direction	Turn	Footwork	Body Alignment
1.	**Right foot** back, diagonally to Wall.	Nil.	Ball flat.	Backing diagonally to Wall.
2.	**Left foot** back, diagonally to Wall.	Nil.	Ball flat.	Backing diagonally to Wall.
3.	**Right foot** back, diagonally to Wall.	Nil.	Ball flat.	Backing diagonally to Wall.
4.	**Left foot** to side, a short step, diagonally to Wall against Line of Dance.	Nil.	Ball flat.	Backing diagonally to Wall.
5.	Tap **right foot** to **left foot**, without weight.	Nil.	Ball.	Backing diagonally to Wall.

Rhythm: Slow – Slow – Quick – Quick – Slow
Calling Cues: Back – Back – Step – Side – Tap
Note: A $\frac{1}{4}$ turn to the left can be made over steps 3 to 5.

Progressive Link

Man's steps

Preparatory Position: Start facing diagonally to Wall, weight on the **right foot**, in Close Hold. End facing diagonally to Wall.

Step	Foot Position and Direction	Turn	Footwork	Body Alignment
1.	**Left foot** forward, diagonally to Wall.	Nil.	Heel flat.	Facing diagonally to Wall.

2.	**Right foot** closes to **left foot**, turning the lady to Promenade position.	Nil.	Ball flat.	Facing diagonally to Wall.
3.	**Left foot** to side, along Line of Dance, in Promenade position.	Nil.	Heel flat.	Facing diagonally to Wall.

Rhythm: Quick – Quick – Slow
Calling Cues: Step – Close – Side

Lady's steps

Preparatory Position: Start backing diagonally to Wall, weight on the **left foot**, in Close Hold. End facing diagonally to Centre in Promenade position.

Step	Foot Position and Direction	Turn	Footwork	Body Alignment
1.	**Right foot** back, diagonally to Wall.	Nil.	Ball flat.	Backing diagonally to Wall.
2.	**Left foot** closes to **right foot**, turning to Promenade position.	¼ to right.	Ball flat.	Facing diagonally to Centre.
3.	**Right foot** to side, along Line of Dance, in Promenade position.	Nil.	Heel flat.	Facing diagonally to Centre.

Rhythm: Quick – Quick – Slow
Calling Cues: Step – Close – Side

Open Turn to Left with a Closed Finish

Man's steps

Preparatory Position: Start facing diagonally to Centre, weight on the **right foot**, in Close Hold. End facing diagonally to Wall.

Step	Foot Position and Direction	Turn	Footwork	Body Alignment
1.	**Left foot** forward, diagonally to Centre.	Body turn to left.	Heel flat.	Facing diagonally to Centre.
2.	**Right foot** to side, diagonally to Centre.	Continue to turn.	Ball flat.	Backing diagonally to Wall.

3.	**Left foot** back, down Line of Dance, partner outside on the right side.	⅜ to left, over steps 1-3.	Ball flat.	Backing Line of Dance.
4.	**Right foot** back, down Line of Dance, partner in line.	Body turn to left.	Ball flat.	Backing Line of Dance.
5.	**Left foot** to side, along Line of Dance.	Continue to turn.	Ball flat.	Foot pointing diagonally to Wall.
6.	Close **right foot** to **left foot**.	⅜ to left, over steps 4-6.	Ball flat.	Facing diagonally to Wall.

Rhythm: Quick – Quick – Slow – Quick – Quick – Slow
Calling Cues: Step – Turn – Back – Back – Turn – Close

Lady's steps

Preparatory Position: Start backing diagonally to Centre, weight on the **left foot**, in Close Hold. End backing diagonally to Wall.

Step	Foot Position and Direction	Turn	Footwork	Body Alignment
1.	**Right foot** back, diagonally to Centre.	Body turn to left.	Ball flat.	Backing diagonally to Centre.
2.	**Left foot** to side, diagonally to Centre.	Continue to turn.	Ball flat.	Foot pointing Line of Dance.
3.	**Right foot** forward, down Line of Dance, outside partner, on partner's right side.	⅜ to left, over steps 1-3.	Heel flat.	Facing Line of Dance.
4.	**Left foot** forward, down Line of Dance, in line with partner.	Body turn to left.	Heel flat.	Facing Line of Dance.
5.	**Right foot** to side, along Line of Dance.	Continue to turn.	Ball flat.	Backing diagonally to Wall.
6.	Close **left foot** to **right foot**.	⅜ to left, over steps 4-6.	Ball flat.	Backing diagonally to Wall.

Rhythm: Quick – Quick – Slow – Quick – Quick – Slow
Calling Cues: Step – Turn – Forward – Step – Turn – Close

Closed Promenade

Man's steps

Preparatory Position: Start facing diagonally to Wall, weight on the **left foot** in Promenade position. End facing diagonally to Wall.

Step	Foot Position and Direction	Turn	Footwork	Body Alignment
1.	**Right foot** forward and across **left foot**, down Line of Dance, in Promenade position.	Nil.	Heel flat.	Facing diagonally to Wall.
2.	**Left foot** to side, along Line of Dance, turning lady to Close Hold.	Nil.	Ball flat.	Facing diagonally to Wall.
3.	Close **right foot** to **left foot**.	Nil.	Ball flat.	Facing diagonally to Wall.

Rhythm: Quick – Quick – Slow
Calling Cues: Step – Step – Close

Lady's steps

Preparatory Position: Start facing diagonally to Centre, weight on the **right foot**, in Promenade position. End backing diagonally to Wall.

Step	Foot Position and Direction	Turn	Footwork	Body Alignment
1.	**Left foot** forward and across **right foot**, down Line of Dance, in Promenade position.	Nil.	Heel flat.	Facing diagonally to Centre.
2.	**Right foot** to side, along Line of Dance, turning square to partner, to end in Close Hold.	Nil.	Ball flat.	Backing diagonally to Wall.
3.	Close **left foot** to **right foot**.	Nil.	Ball flat.	Backing diagonally to Wall.

Rhythm: Quick – Quick – Slow
Calling Cues: Step – Turn – Close

Backward Rock on Left Foot

Man's steps

Preparatory Position: Start backing diagonally to Centre, weight on the **right foot**, in Close Hold. End facing diagonally to Wall.

Step	Foot Position and Direction	Turn	Footwork	Body Alignment
1.	**Left foot** back, a short step, down Line of Dance.	Nil.	Ball flat.	Backing diagonally to Centre
2.	Transfer weight forward to **right foot**, against Line of Dance.	Nil.	Heel flat.	Facing diagonally to Wall against Line of Dance.
3.	**Left foot** back, a short step, down Line of Dance.	Nil.	Ball flat.	Backing diagonally to Centre.
4.	**Right foot** back, diagonally to Centre.	Turn to left.	Ball flat.	Backing diagonally to Centre.
5.	**Left foot** to side, along Line of Dance.	Continue to turn.	Ball flat.	Foot pointing diagonally to Wall.
6.	Close **right foot** to **left foot**.	⅜ to left, over steps 4-6.	Ball flat.	Facing diagonally to Wall.

Rhythm: Quick – Quick – Slow – Quick – Quick – Slow
Calling Cues: Step – Rock – Rock – Step – Turn – Close
Note: Steps 4 to 6 are known as the Closed Finish.

Lady's steps

Preparatory Position: Start facing diagonally to Centre, weight on the **left foot**, in Close Hold. End backing diagonally to Wall.

Step	Foot Position and Direction	Turn	Footwork	Body Alignment
1.	**Right foot** forward, a short step, down Line of Dance.	Nil.	Heel flat.	Facing diagonally to Centre
2.	Transfer weight back to **left foot**, against Line of Dance.	Nil.	Ball flat.	Backing diagonally to Wall against Line of Dance.

3.	**Right foot** forward, a short step, down Line of Dance.	Nil.	Heel flat.	Facing diagonally to Centre.
4.	**Left foot** forward, diagonally to Centre.	Turn to left.	Heel flat.	Facing diagonally to Centre.
5.	**Right foot** to side, along Line of Dance.	Continue to turn.	Ball flat.	Backing diagonally to Wall.
6.	Close **left foot** to **right foot**.	⅜ to left, over steps 4-6.	Ball flat.	Backing diagonally to Wall.

Rhythm: Quick – Quick – Slow – Quick – Quick – Slow
Calling Cues: Step – Rock – Rock – Step – Turn – Close
Note: Steps 4 to 6 are known as the Closed Finish.

Rocking Turn to Right

Man's steps

Preparatory Position: Start facing diagonally to Wall, weight on the **left foot**, in Close Hold. End facing diagonally to Wall.

Step	Foot Position and Direction	Turn	Footwork	Body Alignment
1.	**Right foot** forward, diagonally to Wall.	Body turn to right.	Heel flat.	Facing diagonally to Wall.
2.	**Left foot** to side, a short step, along Line of Dance.	Continue to turn.	Ball flat.	Facing Wall.
3.	Transfer weight forward to **Right foot**, diagonally to Wall against Line of Dance.	¼ to right, over steps 1-3.	Heel flat.	Facing diagonally to Wall against Line of Dance.
4.	Transfer weight back to **left foot**, diagonally to Centre.	Body turn to left.	Ball flat.	Backing diagonally to Centre.
5.	**Right foot** back, diagonally to Centre.	Continue to turn.	Ball flat.	Backing diagonally to Centre.

6.	**Left foot** to side, along Line of Dance.	Continue to turn.	Ball flat.	Foot pointing diagonally to Wall.
7.	Close **right foot** to **left foot**.	¼ to left, over steps 4-7.	Ball flat.	Facing diagonally to Wall.

Rhythm: Slow – Quick – Quick – Slow – Quick – Quick – Slow
Calling Cues: Forward – Side – Rock – Rock – Step – Turn – Close
Note: Steps 4 to 6 are known as the Closed Finish.

Lady's steps

Preparatory Position: Start backing diagonally to Wall, weight on the **right foot**, in Close Hold. End backing diagonally to Wall.

Step	Foot Position and Direction	Turn	Footwork	Body Alignment
1.	**Left foot** back, diagonally to Wall.	Body turn to right.	Ball flat.	Backing diagonally to Wall.
2.	**Right foot** to side, a short step, along Line of Dance, to end between partner's feet.	Continue to turn.	Heel flat.	Facing Centre.
3.	Transfer weight back to **left foot**, diagonally to Wall against Line of Dance.	¼ to right, over steps 1-3.	Ball flat.	Backing diagonally to Wall against Line of Dance.
4.	Transfer weight forward to **right foot**, diagonally to Centre.	Body turn to left.	Heel flat.	Facing diagonally to Centre.
5.	**Left foot** forward, diagonally to Centre.	Continue to turn.	Heel flat.	Facing diagonally to Centre.
6.	**Right foot** to side, along Line of Dance.	Continue to turn.	Ball flat.	Backing diagonally to Wall.
7.	Close **left foot** to **right foot**.	¼ to left, over steps 4-7.	Ball flat.	Backing diagonally to Wall.

Rhythm: Slow – Quick – Quick – Slow – Quick – Quick – Slow
Calling Cues: Back – Side – Rock – Rock – Step – Turn – Close
Note: Steps 4 to 6 are known as the Closed Finish.

Precedes and Follows

Tango Walks to Argentina Close
Before: Tango Walks to Argentina Close, Closed Promenade, Open Turn to Left with a Closed Finish and Backward Rock on the Left Foot.
After: Tango Walks to Argentina Close and Open Turn to Left with a Closed Finish.

Open Turn to Left with a Closed Finish
Before: Tango Walks to Argentina Close.
After: Progressive Link and Tango Walks to Argentina Close.

Closed Promenade
Before: Progressive Link.
After: Tango Walks to Argentina Close and Progressive Link.

Backward Rock on Left Foot
Before: Closed Promenade (man turns to right to finish square to lady). Open Turn to Left with a Closed Finish (man makes no turn over steps 4-6 to end backing diagonally to Centre). Backward Rock on the Left Foot (man makes no turn).
After: Tango Walks to Argentina Close and Progressive Link.

Rocking Turn to Right
Before: Closed Promenade and Open Turn to Left with a Closed Finish, followed by a Left Foot Walk.
After: Tango Walks to Argentina Close and Progressive Link.

Practice Choreography

Routine One
Preparatory Position: Start facing diagonally to Wall, weight on the **right foot**, in Close Hold. End facing diagonally to Wall.
Tango Walks to Argentina Close. Repeat.

Routine Two
Preparatory Position: Start facing diagonally to Wall, weight on the **right foot**, in Close Hold. End facing diagonally to Wall.
Tango Walks to Argentina Close (on the foot tap, turn the lady to Promenade position and step to side with the left foot). Continue with a Closed Promenade, along Line of Dance.

Routine Three
Preparatory Position: Start facing diagonally to Wall, weight on the **right foot**, in Close Hold. End facing diagonally to Wall.
Tango Walks to Argentina Close (on the foot tap, turn the lady to Promenade position and step to side with the left foot). Continue with a Closed Promenade. **Left foot** Walk. Rocking Turn to Right.

Routine Four
Preparatory Position: Start facing diagonally to Centre, weight on the **right foot**, in Close Hold. End facing diagonally to Wall.

Open Turn to Left with a Closed Finish. Tango Walks to Argentina Close (on the foot tap, turn the lady to Promenade position and step to side with the left foot). Continue with a Closed Promenade. **Left foot** Walk. Rocking Turn to Right.

Routine Five
Preparatory Position: Start facing diagonally to Wall, weight on the **right foot**, in Close Hold. End facing diagonally to Wall.

Tango Walks to Argentina Close, making a ¼ turn to left, over steps 3 to 5 to end facing diagonally to Centre. Open Turn to Left with a Closed Finish (man makes no turn over steps 4-6).

Backward Rock on the Left Foot. Tango Walks to Argentina Close. Progressive Link. Closed Promenade. **Left foot** Walk. Rocking Turn to Right.

The Latin Dances

The popularity of the Latin dances is still growing. More than ever before dance schools are receiving enquiries such as 'Do you teach Mambo?' or 'Do you have a class in Merengue?'. The interest that is shown stems from the fact that more people are taking their holidays in places such as Latin America, where these dances developed. At all social dance functions you will be sure to have part of the dance programme devoted to these infectious musical rhythms. With this book you should be able to learn and enjoy the more popular of these Latin dances: Rumba, Samba, Cha Cha Cha, Merengue and Salsa/Mambo.

Promenade position

Underarm turn

Double hold

Wrap position

The Holds

Latin dances have a wide variety of holds that add greatly to their visual appearance. Some of the common ones are illustrated on the facing page and the ones needing more precise explanations are described below.

The Latin Close Hold

The man stands facing and slightly apart from his partner, with his left hand, palm to palm, holding the lady's right hand between his first finger and thumb with his fingers wrapped lightly around the lady's right hand. The joined left and right hands are held vertical with the hand approximately level to the man's left ear. The man places his right hand across the lady's left shoulder blade his right forearm is parallel to the floor. The lady's left hand is placed in a comfortable position on the man's right shoulder. This hold is known as the Latin Hold.

The Open Promenade Position Hold (OPP)

When the man's left side and the lady's right side are turned open to form a 'V' shape. The man's right hand is holding the lady's left hand. The free hands are held slightly to the side.

The Open Counter Promenade Position Hold (OCPP)

When the man's right side and the lady's left side are turned open to form a 'V' shape. The man's left hand is holding the lady's right hand. The free hands are held slightly to the side.

The Rhythm or Timing

The music is divided into bars with each bar holding 2, 3 or 4 beats. You will normally find that the first beat in the bar of music is accented, which invites you to take your first step. When you are first learning to dance, dancing to the music can prove to be difficult. Some people have no difficulty in picking out the accented beats, while others do seem to be deaf to the rhythm. This can be overcome by constantly listening to the music and trying to hear the accented beat, which will always be the stronger of the beats.

Merengue

Time signature: 2/4; two beats to the bar.

Rhythm: Unless stated, each step takes one beat of music.

Tempo: Approximately 60 bars per minute. (120 mm.)

The Merengue is the most popular dance throughout the Caribbean and South America. In the European countries the dance has gained in popularity because of the easy figuration and infectious rhythm. People who have visited the Caribbean on holiday return to say the music of the Merengue can be heard day and night throughout the islands. Because the origin of the dance is Spanish, the figuration of the Merengue can be danced to Paso Doble music.

Alignments

In the progressive dances (Merengue, Samba) it is necessary to have alignments so that the couples dancing can move around the floor without being a hindrance to one another. The dancer moving forward normally has a facing alignment and the dancer moving backwards a backing alignment.

In the non-progressive dances alignments are not necessary. In these non-progressive dances I have written the body alignment for the sole purpose of learning the figure, with the man and lady commencing the figure in a facing alignment i.e. man facing Wall, lady facing Centre. It should go without saying that the figures could be commenced on any alignment.

The New Holds

Fallaway Position
When the man's left side and the lady's right side are turned open to form a 'V' shape. The man or the lady steps back, the position is then known as Fallaway.

Promenade Position
This is as Fallaway Position, but the man or lady steps forward.

Basic Movement in Place

Man's steps

Preparatory Position: Start facing Wall, weight on **left foot**, in Close Hold. End facing Wall.

Step	Foot Position and Direction	Turn	Footwork	Body Alignment
1.	**Right foot**, in place.	Nil, or turned to the right or the left.	Ball flat.	Facing Wall.
2.	**Left foot**, in place.		Ball flat.	Facing Wall.

3.	**Right foot**, in place.		Ball flat.	Facing Wall.
4.	**Left foot**, in place.		Ball flat.	Facing Wall.

Rhythm: 1 – 2 – 1 – 2
Calling Cues: Mark – Time – Mark – Time

Lady's steps

Preparatory Position: Start backing Wall, weight on **right foot**, in Close Hold. End backing Wall.

Step	Foot Position and Direction	Turn	Footwork	Body Alignment
1.	**Left foot**, in place.	Nil, or turned to the right or the left.	Ball flat.	Backing Wall.
2.	**Right foot**, in place.		Ball flat.	Backing Wall.
3.	**Left foot**, in place.		Ball flat.	Backing Wall.
4.	**Right foot**, in place.		Ball flat.	Backing Wall.

Rhythm: 1 – 2 – 1 – 2
Calling Cues: Mark – Time – Mark – Time

Basic Side Step to Left

Man's steps

Preparatory Position: Start facing Wall, weight on **right foot**, in Close Hold. End facing Wall.

Step	Foot Position and Direction	Turn	Footwork	Body Alignment
1.	**Left foot** to side, along Line of Dance.	Nil.	Ball flat.	Facing Wall.
2.	Close **right foot** to **left foot**.	Nil.	Ball flat.	Facing Wall.
3.	**Left foot** to side, along Line of Dance.	Nil.	Ball flat.	Facing Wall.
4.	Close **right foot** to **left foot**.	Nil.	Ball flat.	Facing Wall.

Rhythm: 1 – 2 – 1 – 2
Calling Cues: Side – Close – Side – Close

Lady's steps

Preparatory Position: Start backing Wall, weight on **left foot**, in Close Hold. End backing Wall.

Step	Foot Position and Direction	Turn	Footwork	Body Alignment
1.	**Right foot** to side, along Line of Dance.	Nil.	Ball flat.	Backing Wall.
2.	Close **left foot** to **right foot**.	Nil.	Ball flat.	Backing Wall.
3.	**Right foot** to side, along Line of Dance.	Nil.	Ball flat.	Backing Wall.
4.	Close **left foot** to **right foot**.	Nil.	Ball flat.	Backing Wall.

Rhythm: 1 – 2 – 1 – 2
Calling Cues: Side – Close – Side – Close

Basic Side Step to Right

Man's steps

Preparatory Position: Start facing Centre, weight on **left foot**, in Close Hold. End facing Centre.

Step	Foot Position and Direction	Turn	Footwork	Body Alignment
1.	**Right foot** to side, along Line of Dance.	Nil.	Ball flat.	Facing Centre.
2.	Close **left foot** to **right foot**.	Nil.	Ball flat.	Facing Centre.
3.	**Right foot** to side, along Line of Dance.	Nil.	Ball flat.	Facing Centre.
4.	Close **left foot** to **right foot**.	Nil.	Ball flat.	Facing Centre.

Rhythm: 1 – 2 – 1 – 2
Calling Cues: Side – Close – Side – Close

Lady's steps

Preparatory Position: Start backing Centre, weight on **right foot**, in Close Hold. End backing Centre.

Step	Foot Position and Direction	Turn	Footwork	Body Alignment
1.	**Left foot** to side, along Line of Dance.	Nil.	Ball flat.	Backing Centre.

2.	Close **right foot** to **left foot**.	Nil.	Ball flat.	Backing Centre.
3.	**Left foot** to side, along Line of Dance.	Nil.	Ball flat.	Backing Centre.
4.	Close **right foot** to **left foot**.	Nil.	Ball flat.	Backing Centre.

Rhythm: 1 – 2 – 1 – 2
Calling Cues: Side – Close – Side – Close

Basic Walk on the Right Foot

Man's steps

Preparatory Position: Start facing Line of Dance, weight on **left foot**, in Close Hold. End facing Line of Dance.

Step	Foot Position and Direction	Turn	Footwork	Body Alignment
1.	**Right foot** forward, a short step, down Line of Dance.	Nil or slight turn to right or left, over steps 1-4.	Ball flat.	Facing Line of Dance.
2.	Close or almost close **left foot** to **right foot**.		Ball flat.	Facing Line of Dance.
3.	**Right foot** forward, a short step, down Line of Dance.		Ball flat.	Facing Line of Dance.
4.	Close or almost close **left foot** to **right foot**.		Ball flat.	Facing Line of Dance.

Rhythm: 1 – 2 – 1 – 2
Calling Cues: Step – Close – Step – Close

Lady's steps

Preparatory Position: Start backing Line of Dance, weight on **right foot**, in Close Hold. End backing Line of Dance.

Step	Foot Position and Direction	Turn	Footwork	Body Alignment
1.	**Left foot** back, a short step, down Line of Dance.	Nil or slight turn to right or left, over steps 1-4.	Ball flat.	Backing Line of Dance.

2.	Close or almost close **right foot** to **left foot**.		Ball flat.	Backing Line of Dance.
3.	**Left foot** back, a short step, down Line of Dance.		Ball flat.	Backing Line of Dance.
4.	Close or almost close **right foot** to **left foot**.		Ball flat.	Backing Line of Dance.

Rhythm: 1 – 2 – 1 – 2
Calling Cues: Step – Close – Step – Close

Merengue Square

Man's steps

Preparatory Position: Start facing Line of Dance, weight on **right foot**, in Close Hold. End facing Line of Dance.

Step	Foot Position and Direction	Turn	Footwork	Body Alignment
1.	**Left foot** forward, a short step, down Line of Dance.	Nil.	Ball flat.	Facing Line of Dance.
2.	**Right foot** to side, to Wall.	Nil.	Ball flat.	Facing Line of Dance
3.	Close **left foot** to **right foot**.	Nil.	Ball flat.	Facing Line of Dance.
4.	**Right foot** back, against Line of Dance.	Nil.	Ball flat.	Backing against Line of Dance.
5.	**Left foot** to side, to Centre.	Nil.	Ball flat.	Backing against Line of Dance.
6.	Close **right foot** to **left foot**.	Nil.	Ball flat.	Facing Line of Dance.

Rhythm: 1 – 2 – 1 – 2 – 1 – 2
Calling Cues: Step – Side – Close – Step – Side – Close

Lady's steps

Preparatory Position: Start backing Line of Dance, weight on **left foot**, in Close Hold. End backing Line of Dance.

Step	Foot Position and Direction	Turn	Footwork	Body Alignment
1.	**Right foot** back, short step, down Line of Dance.	Nil.	Ball flat.	Backing Line of Dance.
2.	**Left foot** to side, to Wall.	Nil.	Ball flat.	Backing Line of Dance.
3.	Close **right foot** to **left foot**.	Nil.	Ball flat.	Backing Line of Dance.
4.	**Left foot** forward, against Line of Dance.	Nil.	Ball flat.	Facing against Line of Dance.
5.	**Right foot** to side, to Centre.	Nil.	Ball flat.	Facing against Line of Dance.
6.	Close **left foot** to **right foot**.	Nil.	Ball flat.	Backing Line of Dance.

Rhythm: 1 – 2 – 1 – 2 – 1 – 2
Calling Cues: Step – Side – Close – Step – Side – Close

The Left Foot Basic Step in Fallaway

Man's steps

Preparatory Position: Start facing Wall, weight on **right foot**, in Close Hold. End facing Wall.

Step	Foot Position and Direction	Turn	Footwork	Body Alignment
1.	**Left foot** to the side, a short step, along Line of Dance.	Nil.	Ball flat.	Facing Wall.
2.	Close **right foot** to **left foot**.	Nil.	Ball flat.	Facing Wall.
3.	**Left foot** to the side, a short step, along Line of Dance.	Nil.	Ball flat.	Facing Wall.
4.	Close **right foot** to **left foot**.	Nil.	Ball flat.	Facing Wall.

5.	Turning to left, **left foot** back, against Line of Dance, in Fallaway Position.	⅛ to left.	Ball flat.	Facing diagonally to Wall.
6.	Replace weight forward to **right foot**, down Line of Dance, in Promenade position.	Nil.	Ball flat.	Facing diagonally to Wall.
7.	Turning to right, **left foot** to the side, along Line of Dance, square to partner.	⅛ to right.	Ball flat.	Facing Wall.
8.	Close **right foot** to **left foot**.	Nil.	Ball flat.	Facing Wall.

Rhythm: 1 – 2 – 1 – 2 – 1 – 2 – 1 – 2
Calling Cues: Step – Close – Step – Close – Back – Replace – Turn – Close

Lady's steps

Preparatory Position: Start backing Wall, weight on **left foot**, in Close Hold. End backing Wall.

Step	Foot Position and Direction	Turn	Footwork	Body Alignment
1.	**Right foot** to the side, a short step, along Line of Dance.	Nil.	Ball flat.	Backing Wall.
2.	Close **left foot** to **right foot**.	Nil.	Ball flat.	Backing Wall.
3.	**Right foot** to the side, a short step, along Line of Dance.	Nil.	Ball flat.	Backing Wall.
4.	Close **left foot** to **right foot**.	Nil.	Ball flat.	Backing Wall.
5.	**Right foot** back, against Line of Dance, in Fallaway Position.	⅛ to right.	Ball flat.	Facing diagonally to Centre.
6.	Replace weight forward to **left foot**, down Line of Dance, in Promenade position.	Nil.	Ball flat.	Facing diagonally to Centre.
7.	**Right foot** to the side, along Line of Dance, square to partner.	⅛ to left.	Ball flat.	Backing Wall.
8.	Close **left foot** to **right foot**.	Nil.	Ball flat.	Backing Wall.

Rhythm: 1 – 2 – 1 – 2 – 1 – 2 – 1 – 2
Calling Cues: Step – Close – Step – Close – Back – Replace – Turn – Close

Underarm Turn to Right

Man's steps

Preparatory Position: Start facing Wall, weight on **right foot**, the joined hands raised. End facing Wall in Closed Hold.

Hold: The man raises his left and lady's right hand above the heads, indicating to the lady with his right hand to turn under the raised arms to the right. He then releases hold with the right hand, regaining Close Hold on step 8.

Step	Foot Position and Direction	Turn	Footwork	Body Alignment
1-8.	Dance a **Basic Movement in Place**, commencing with the **Left foot**.	No turn.	Ball flat on each step.	Facing Wall, throughout.

Rhythm: 1 – 2 – 1 – 2 – 1 – 2 – 1 – 2
Calling Cues: Mark – Time – Mark – Time – Mark – Time – Mark – Time

Lady's steps

Preparatory Position: Start backing Wall, weight on **left foot**, the joined hands raised. End backing Wall in Closed Hold.

Hold: The lady's right hand is raised above the heads. She releases hold with the left hand as she turns to the right under the raised arms, regaining Close Hold on step 8.

Step	Foot Position and Direction	Turn	Footwork	Body Alignment
1-8.	Dance a Basic **Right Foot Walk**, for 8 counts, moving in a clockwise direction under the raised arms.	One full turn to right, over steps 1-8.	Ball flat, on each step.	Backing Wall, end backing Wall.

Rhythm: 1 – 2 – 1 – 2 – 1 – 2 – 1 – 2
Calling Cues: Step – Close – Step – Close – Step – Close – Step – Close

Underarm Turn to Left

Man's steps

Preparatory Position: Start facing Wall, weight on **right foot**, the joined hands raised. End in Close hold.

Hold: The man raises his left and lady's right hand above the heads Releasing hold with the right hand, he then turns to the left under the raised arms, regaining Close Hold on step 8.

Step	Foot Position and Direction	Turn	Footwork	Body Alignment
1-8.	Dance a Basic **Left Foot** Walk, for 8 counts, turning in an anti-clockwise direction under the raised arms.	One full turn to left, over steps 1-8.	Ball flat, on each step.	Facing Wall, end facing Wall.

Rhythm: 1 – 2 – 1 – 2 – 1 – 2 – 1 – 2
Calling Cues: Step – Close – Step – Close – Step – Close – Step – Close
Note: A Left Foot Basic Walk has the same technique as a Right Foot Basic Walk but turning to the left.

Lady's steps

Preparatory Position: Start backing Wall, weight on **left foot**, the joined hands raised. End in Close hold.

Hold: The lady's right hand is raised above the heads. She releases hold with the left hand as the man turns to the left under the raised arms. She regains Close Hold on step 8.

Step	Foot Position and Direction	Turn	Footwork	Body Alignment
1-8.	Dance a **Basic Movement in Place**, commencing with the **right foot**.	No turn.	Ball flat, on each step.	Backing Wall, throughout.

Rhythm: 1 – 2 – 1 – 2 – 1 – 2 – 1 – 2
Calling Cues: Mark – Time – Mark – Time – Mark – Time – Mark – Time

Precedes and Follows

Basic Movement in Place
Before: Basic Movement in Place, Basic Side Step to Right and Basic Walk on Right Foot.
After: Basic Movement in Place, Basic Side Step to Right and Basic Walk on Right Foot.

Basic Side Step to Left
Before: Basic Side Step to Left, Merengue Square, The Left Foot Basic Side Step in Fallaway, Underarm Turn to Left and Underarm Turn to Right.
After: Basic Side Step to Left, Merengue Square, The Left Foot Basic Side Step in Fallaway, Underarm Turn to Left and Underarm Turn to Right.

Basic Side Step to Right
Before: Basic Movement in Place, Basic Side Step to Right and Basic Walk on Right Foot.
After: Basic Movement in Place, Basic Side Step to Right and Basic Walk on Right Foot.

Basic Walk on the Right Foot
Before: Basic Walk on the Right Foot, Basic Movement in Place and Basic Side Step to Right.
After: Basic Walk on the Right Foot, Basic Movement in Place and Basic Side Step to Right.

Merengue Square
Before: Basic Side Step to Left, Merengue Square, The Left Foot Basic Side Step in Fallaway, Underarm Turn to Left and Underarm Turn to the Right.
After: Basic Side Step to Left, Merengue Square, The Left Foot Basic Side Step in Fallaway, Underarm Turn to Left and Underarm Turn to the Right.

The Left Foot Basic Step in Fallaway
Before: Basic Side Step to Left, Merengue Square, The Left Foot Basic Side Step in Fallaway, Underarm Turn to Left and Underarm Turn to the Right.
After: Basic Side Step to Left, Merengue Square, The Left Foot Basic Side Step in Fallaway, Underarm Turn to Left and Underarm Turn to the Right.

Underarm Turn to Right
Before: Basic Side Step to Left, Merengue Square, The Left Foot Basic Side Step in Fallaway, Underarm Turn to Left and Underarm Turn to the Right.
After: Basic Movement in Place, Basic Side Step to Right, Basic Walk on Right Foot, Underarm Turn to Right and Underarm Turn to the Left.

Underarm Turn to Left
Before: Basic Side Step to Left, Merengue Square, The Left Foot Basic Side Step in Fallaway, Underarm Turn to Left and Underarm Turn to the Right.
After: Basic Side Step to Left, Merengue Square, The Left Foot Basic Side Step in Fallaway, Underarm Turn to Left and Underarm Turn to the Right.

Practice Choreography

Note: In order to achieve a particular alignment, either more or less turn can be made on a figure and figures that are standardised without turn can also be turned to the right or to the left.

Routine One

Preparatory Position: Start facing Wall, weight on the **left foot**, in Close Hold. End facing Line of Dance.
Dance 1-8 of the Basic Movement in Place, turning to face Line of Dance. Dance 1-8 of the Basic Walk on the Right Foot.

Routine Two

Preparatory Position: Start facing Line of Dance, weight on the **left foot**, in Close Hold. End facing Centre.
Dance 1-8 of the Basic Walk on the Right Foot, making a ¼ turn to the left on step 8. Basic Side Step to Right.

Routine Three

Preparatory Position: Start facing Centre, weight on the **left foot**, in Close Hold. End facing Wall.
Dance 1-8 of the Basic Side Step to Right. Dance 1-8 Basic Movement in Place, turning ½ to right to end facing Wall. Dance 1-8 of the Basic Movement in Place, closing without weight on count 8. Basic Side Step to Left.

Routine Four

Preparatory Position: Start facing Wall, weight on the **right foot**, in Close Hold. End facing Wall.
Dance 1-6 of the Merengue Square. Dance 1-8 of the Basic Side Step to Left. Dance 1-6 of the Merengue Square. Left Foot Basic Step in Fallaway.

Routine Five

Preparatory Position: Start facing Wall, weight on the **right foot**, in Close Hold. End facing Wall.
Left Foot Basic Step in Fallaway. Basic Side Step to Left. Underarm Turn to Left. Dance 1-8 of the Basic Side Step to Left. Underarm Turn to Right.

Latin rhythms are widely used in popular music: Gloria Estefan is one of the best-known interpreters, but there are many more, including Madonna!

Cha Cha Cha

Time signature: 4/4; four beats to the bar.

Rhythm: As a social dance, the first beat in each bar is accented. Count 1-2-3-4-&-1. More 'correct' dancers emphasise the second beat in each bar.

Tempo: Music should be played at about 34 bars per minute. (136mm.)

The Cha Cha Cha is one of the later additions to the Latin dances. It was first seen in the early 1950s in the clubs of South America. Its origin can be traced to the Mambo, and the Cha Cha Cha and is often referred to as the Triple Mambo because of the rhythm that synchronises with the musical count of 1-2-3-4 & 1. When calling the timing of the dance, the 4 & 1 counts become Cha Cha Cha, with a beat value of $\frac{1}{2}$, $\frac{1}{2}$, 1 beat. Today the dance is often called the Cha Cha, to coincide with the two half beats.

Action

On each step that occupies a full beat of music, a hip action is used in the direction in which the step is taken i.e. **Left foot** forward, hip moves to the left. Replace weight to **right foot**, hip moves to the right. No noticeable hip action is used on the Cha Cha.

The New Holds

Right Side-by-Side
When the man and lady are standing side-by-side, the man's right shoulder adjacent to the lady's left shoulder, both facing the same way.

Left Side-by-Side
When the man and lady are standing side-by-side, the man's left shoulder adjacent to the lady's right shoulder, both facing the same way.

Right Foot Basic in Place

Man's steps
Preparatory Position: Start facing Wall, weight on **left foot**, in Close Hold. End facing Wall.

Step	Foot Position and Direction	Turn	Footwork	Body Alignment
1.	**Right foot** to the side, a short step, against Line of Dance.	Nil.	Ball flat.	Facing Wall.
2.	Close **left foot** to **right foot**.	Nil.	Ball flat.	Facing Wall.

3.	Replace weight to **right foot**, in place.	Nil.	Ball flat.	Facing Wall.
4.	**Left foot** to the side, a short step, along Line of Dance.	Nil.	Ball flat.	Facing Wall.
5.	Close **right foot** towards **left foot**.	Nil.	Ball flat.	Facing Wall.

Rhythm: 1 – 2 – 3 – 4 – &
Calling Cues: Side – Mark – Time – Cha – Cha

Lady's steps

Preparatory Position: Start facing Centre, weight on **right foot**, in Close Hold. End facing Centre.

Step	Foot Position and Direction	Turn	Footwork	Body Alignment
1.	**Left foot**, to the side, a short step, against Line of Dance.	Nil.	Ball flat.	Facing Centre.
2.	Close **right foot** to **left foot**.	Nil.	Ball flat.	Facing Centre.
3.	Replace weight to **left foot**, in place.	Nil.	Ball flat.	Facing Centre.
4.	**Right foot** to the side, a short step, along Line of Dance.	Nil.	Ball flat.	Facing Centre.
5.	Close **left foot** towards **right foot**.	Nil.	Ball flat.	Facing Centre.

Rhythm: 1 – 2 – 3 – 4 – &
Calling Cues: Side – Mark – Time – Cha – Cha

Left Foot Basic in Place

Man's steps

Preparatory Position: Start facing Wall, weight on **right foot**, in Close Hold. End facing Wall.

Step	Foot Position and Direction	Turn	Footwork	Body Alignment
1.	**Left foot**, to the side, a short step, along Line of Dance.	Nil.	Ball flat.	Facing Wall.
2.	Close **right foot** to **left foot**.	Nil.	Ball flat.	Facing Wall.
3.	Replace weight to **left foot**, in place.	Nil.	Ball flat.	Facing Wall.

4.	**Right foot** to the side, a short step, against Line of Dance.	Nil.	Ball flat.	Facing Wall.
5.	Close **left foot** towards **right foot**.	Nil.	Ball flat.	Facing Wall.

Rhythm: 1 – 2 – 3 – 4 – &
Calling Cues: Side – Mark – Time – Cha – Cha

Lady's steps

Preparatory Position: Start facing Centre, weight on **left foot**, in Close Hold. End facing Centre.

Step	Foot Position and Direction	Turn	Footwork	Body Alignment
1.	**Right foot** to the side, a short step, along Line of Dance.	Nil.	Ball flat.	Facing Centre.
2.	Close **left foot** to **right foot**.	Nil.	Ball flat.	Facing Centre.
3.	Replace weight to **right foot**, in place.	Nil.	Ball flat.	Facing Centre.
4.	**Left foot** to the side, a short step, against Line of Dance.	Nil.	Ball flat.	Facing Centre.
5.	Close **right foot** towards **left foot**.	Nil.	Ball flat.	Facing Centre.

Rhythm: 1 – 2 – 3 – 4 – &
Calling Cues: Side – Mark – Time – Cha – Cha

Underarm Turn to Right
Man's steps

Preparatory Position: Start facing Wall, weight on **right foot**, in Close Hold. End facing Wall.

Step	Foot Position and Direction	Turn	Footwork	Body Alignment
1-5.	Dance 1-5 of **Left Foot** Basic in Place.	Nil.	Ball flat, over steps 1-5.	Facing Wall, throughout.

Rhythm: 1 – 2 – 3 – 4 – &
Calling Cues: Side – Mark – Time – Cha – Cha

Hold: The man raises his left and the lady's right hand above the heads, indicating to the lady with his right hand to turn under the raised arms to the right. He then releases hold with the right hand, regaining Close Hold on step 5.

Lady's steps

Preparatory Position: Start facing Centre, weight on **left foot**, in Close Hold.
End facing Centre.

Step	Foot Position and Direction	Turn	Footwork	Body Alignment
1.	**Right foot** to side, along Line of Dance.	Turn to right.	Ball flat.	Foot pointing to Line of Dance.
2.	**Left foot** forward, down line of Dance.	Continue to turn.	Ball flat.	Facing Line of Dance.
3.	Replace weight forward to **right foot**, diagonally to Wall against Line of Dance.	Continue to turn.	Ball flat.	Facing diagonally to Wall against Line of Dance.
4.	**Left foot** to side, against Line of Dance.	Complete turn to right, over steps 1-4.	Ball flat.	Facing Centre.
5.	Close **right foot** towards **left foot**.		Ball flat.	Facing Centre.

Rhythm: 1 – 2 – 3 – 4 – &
Calling Cues: Side – Step – Turn – Cha – Cha
Hold: The lady's right hand is raised above the heads. She releases hold with
the left hand as she turns to the right under the raised arms, regaining Close
Hold on step 5.

Forward Basic Movement

Man's steps

Preparatory Position: Start facing Wall, weight on **left foot**, in Close Hold.
End facing Wall.

Step	Foot Position and Direction	Turn	Footwork	Body Alignment
1.	**Right foot** to side, a short step, against Line of Dance.	Nil.	Ball flat.	Facing Wall.
2.	**Left foot** forward, to wall.	Nil.	Ball flat.	Facing Wall.

3.	Replace weight back to **right foot**, in place.	Nil.	Ball flat.	Backing Centre.
4.	**Left foot** to side, a short step, along line of Dance.	Nil.	Ball flat.	Backing Centre.
5.	Close **right foot** towards **left foot**.	Nil.	Ball flat.	Facing Wall.

Rhythm: 1 – 2 – 3 – 4 – &
Calling Cues: Side – Step – Rock – Cha – Cha

Lady's steps

Preparatory Position: Start facing Centre, weight on **right foot**, in Close Hold. End facing Centre.

Step	Foot Position and Direction	Turn	Footwork	Body Alignment
1.	**Left foot** to side, a short step, against Line of Dance.	Nil.	Ball flat.	Facing Centre.
2.	**Right foot** back, to wall.	Nil.	Ball flat.	Backing Wall.
3.	Replace weight forward to **left foot**, in place.	Nil.	Ball flat.	Facing Centre.
4.	**Right foot** to side, a short step, along line of Dance.	Nil.	Ball flat.	Facing Centre.
5.	Close **left foot** towards **right foot**.	Nil.	Ball flat.	Facing Centre.

Rhythm: 1 – 2 – 3 – 4 – &
Calling Cues: Side – Step – Rock – Cha – Cha

Backward Basic Movement

Man's steps

Preparatory Position: Start facing Wall, weight on **right foot**, in Close Hold. End facing Wall.

Step	Foot Position and Direction	Turn	Footwork	Body Alignment
1.	**Left foot** to side, a short step, along Line of Dance.	Nil.	Ball flat.	Facing Wall.
2.	**Right foot** back , to Centre.	Nil.	Ball flat.	Backing Centre.
3.	Replace weight forward to **left foot**, in place.	Nil.	Ball flat.	Facing Wall.

4.	**Right foot** to side, a short step, against Line of Dance.	Nil.	Ball flat.	Facing Wall.
5.	Close **left foot** towards **right foot**.	Nil.	Ball flat.	Facing Wall.

Rhythm: 1 – 2 – 3 – 4 – &
Calling Cues: Side – Step – Rock – Cha – Cha

Lady's steps

Preparatory Position: Start facing Centre, weight on **left foot**, in Close Hold. End facing Centre.

Step	Foot Position and Direction	Turn	Footwork	Body Alignment
1.	**Right foot** to side, a short step, along Line of Dance.	Nil.	Ball flat.	Facing Centre.
2.	**Left foot** forward, to Centre.	Nil.	Ball flat.	Facing Centre.
3.	Replace weight back to **right foot**, in place.	Nil.	Ball flat.	Backing Wall.
4.	**Left foot** to side, a short step, against Line of Dance.	Nil.	Ball flat.	Facing Centre.
5.	Close **right foot** towards **left foot**.	Nil.	Ball flat.	Facing Centre.

Rhythm: 1 – 2 – 3 – 4 – &
Calling Cues: Side – Step – Rock – Cha – Cha

New Yorker

Man's steps

Preparatory Position: Start facing Wall, weight on **left foot**, in Close Hold. End facing Wall.

Step	Foot Position and Direction	Turn	Footwork	Body Alignment
1.	**Right foot** to the side, a short step, against Line of Dance.	⅛ to right.	Ball flat.	Facing diagonally to Wall against Line of Dance.
2.	**Left foot** forward, over **right foot** and check, against Line of Dance, in OCPP.	⅛ to right.	Ball flat.	Facing against Line of Dance.

3.	Replace weight back to **right foot**, in place.	Turning to left.	Ball flat.	Backing Line of Dance.
4.	**Left foot** to the side, along line of Dance.	$\frac{1}{4}$ to left, over steps 3-4.	Ball flat.	Facing Wall.
5.	Close **right foot** towards **left foot**.	Nil.	Ball flat.	Facing Wall.
6.	**Left foot** to the side, a short step, along line of Dance.	$\frac{1}{8}$ to left.	Ball flat.	Facing diagonally to Wall.
7.	**Right foot** forward, over **left foot** and check, along line of Dance, in OPP.	$\frac{1}{8}$ to left.	Ball flat.	Facing Line of Dance.
8.	Replace weight back to **left foot**, in place.	Turning to right.	Ball flat.	Backing Line of Dance.
9.	**Right foot** to the side, against Line of Dance.	$\frac{1}{4}$ to right, over steps 8-9.	Ball flat.	Facing Wall.
10.	Close **left foot** towards **right foot**.	Nil.	Ball flat.	Facing Wall.

Rhythm: 1 – 2 – 3 – 4 – & – 1 – 2 – 3 – 4 – &
Calling Cues: Side – Check – Rock – Cha – Cha – Side – Check – Rock – Cha – Cha
Hold: The man releases the lady with his right hand on step 2, retaining hold of the lady's right hand. On step 4 he takes the lady's left hand in his right hand to end in Double Hold. The man releases the lady's right hand on step 7, retaining hold of the lady's left hand. On step 9 he regains Close Hold.

Lady's steps

Preparatory Position: Start backing Wall, weight on **right foot**, in Close Hold. End facing Centre.

Step	Foot Position and Direction	Turn	Footwork	Body Alignment
1.	**Left foot** to the side, a short step, against Line of Dance.	$\frac{1}{8}$ to left.	Ball flat.	Facing diagonally to Centre against Line of Dance.
2.	**Right foot** forward, over **left foot** and check, against Line of Dance, OCPP.	$\frac{1}{8}$ to left.	Ball flat.	Facing against Line of Dance.

3.	Replace weight back to **left foot**, in place.	Turning to right.	Ball flat.	Backing Line of Dance.
4.	**Right foot** to the side, along line of Dance.	$\frac{1}{4}$ to right, over steps 3-4.	Ball flat.	Facing Centre.
5.	Close **left foot** towards **right foot**.	Nil.	Ball flat.	Facing Centre.
6.	**Right foot** to the side, a short step, along line of Dance.	$\frac{1}{8}$ to right.	Ball flat.	Facing diagonally to Centre.
7.	**Left foot** forward, over **right foot** and check, down Line of Dance, in OPP.	$\frac{1}{8}$ to right.	Ball flat.	Facing Line of Dance.
8.	Replace weight back to **right foot**, in place.	Turning to left.	Ball flat.	Backing Line of Dance.
9.	**Left foot** to the side, against Line of Dance.	$\frac{1}{4}$ to left, over steps 8-9.	Ball flat.	Facing Centre.
10.	Close **right foot** towards **left foot**.	Nil.	Ball flat.	Facing Centre.

Rhythm: 1 – 2 – 3 – 4 – & – 1 – 2 – 3 – 4 – &
Calling Cues: Side – Check – Rock – Cha – Cha – Side – Check – Rock – Cha – Cha
Hold: The lady releases hold with her left hand on step 2, retaining hold of the man's left hand. On step 4 she joins her left hand to the man's right hand to end in Double Hold. The lady releases hold with her right hand on step 7, retaining hold of the man's right hand. On step 9 she regains Close Hold.

Whisk to Right

Man's steps

Preparatory Position: Start facing Wall, weight on **left foot**, in Close Hold. End facing Wall.

Step	Foot Position and Direction	Turn	Footwork	Body Alignment
1.	**Right foot** to the side, a short step, against Line of Dance.	Nil.	Ball flat.	Facing Wall.
2.	Cross **left foot** behind **right foot** and check, diagonally to Centre against Line of Dance.	$\frac{1}{8}$ to left.	Ball flat.	Backing diagonally to Centre against Line of Dance

3.	Replace weight forward to **right foot**, in place.	Turning to right.	Ball flat.	Facing diagonally to Wall.
4.	**Left foot** to the side, along Line of Dance.	$\frac{1}{8}$ to right, over steps 3-4.	Ball flat.	Facing Wall.
5.	Close **right foot** towards **left foot**.	Nil.	Ball flat.	Facing Wall.

Rhythm: 1 – 2 – 3 – 4 – &
Calling Cues: Side – Cross- Rock – Cha – Cha
Hold: The man can release the lady's right hand on step 2, regaining Close Hold on step 4. The right hand remains on the lady's back.

Lady's steps

Preparatory Position: Start facing Centre, weight on **right foot**, in Close Hold. End facing Centre.

Step	Foot Position and Direction	Turn	Footwork	Body Alignment
1.	**Left foot** to the side, a short step, against Line of Dance.	Nil.	Ball flat.	Facing Centre.
2.	Cross **right foot** behind **left foot** and check, diagonally to Wall against Line of Dance.	$\frac{1}{8}$ to right.	Ball flat.	Backing diagonally to Wall against Line of Dance
3.	Replace weight forward to **left foot**, in place.	Turning to left.	Ball flat.	Facing diagonally to Centre.
4.	**Right foot** to the side, along Line of Dance.	$\frac{1}{8}$ to left, over steps 3-4.	Ball flat.	Facing Centre.
5.	Close **left foot** towards **right foot**.	Nil.	Ball flat.	Facing Centre.

Rhythm: 1 – 2 – 3 – 4 – &
Calling Cues: Side – Cross- Rock – Cha – Cha
Hold: The man can release the lady's right hand on step 2, regaining Close Hold on step 4. The right hand remains on the lady's back.

Whisk to Left

Man's steps

Preparatory Position: Start facing Wall, weight on **right foot**, in Close Hold. End facing Wall.

Step	Foot Position and Direction	Turn	Footwork	Body Alignment
1.	**Left foot** to the side, a short step, along Line of Dance.	Nil.	Ball flat.	Facing Wall.
2.	Cross **right foot** behind **left foot** and check, diagonally to Centre.	⅛ to right.	Ball flat.	Backing diagonally to Centre.
3.	Replace weight forward to **left foot**, in place.	Turning to left.	Ball flat.	Facing diagonally to Wall against Line of Dance.
4.	**Right foot** to the side, against Line of Dance.	⅛ to left, over steps 3-4.	Ball flat.	Facing Wall.
5.	Close **left foot** towards **right foot**.	Nil.	Ball flat.	Facing Wall.

Rhythm: 1 – 2 – 3 – 4 – &
Calling Cues: Side – Cross- Rock – Cha – Cha
Hold: The man can release the lady's right hand on step 2, placing his left hand on the lady's back and releasing hold with his right hand, regaining Close Hold on step 4.

Lady's steps

Preparatory Position: Start facing Centre, weight on **left foot**, in Close Hold. End facing Centre.

Step	Foot Position and Direction	Turn	Footwork	Body Alignment
1.	**Right foot** to the side, a short step, along Line of Dance.	Nil.	Ball flat.	Facing Centre.
2.	Cross **left foot** behind **right foot** and check, diagonally to Wall.	⅛ to left.	Ball flat.	Backing diagonally to Wall.
3.	Replace weight forward to **right foot**, in place.	Turning to right.	Ball flat.	Facing diagonally to Centre against Line of Dance.

4.	Left foot to the side, against Line of Dance.	⅛ to right, over steps 3-4.	Ball flat.	Facing Centre.
5.	Close right foot towards left foot.	Nil.	Ball flat.	Facing Centre.

Rhythm: 1 – 2 – 3 – 4 – &
Calling Cues: Side – Cross- Rock – Cha – Cha
Hold: The man can release the lady's right hand on step 2, placing his left hand on the lady's back and releasing hold with his right hand, regaining Close Hold on step 4.

Hand to Hand

Man's steps

Preparatory Position: Start facing Wall, weight on **left foot**, in Double Hold. End facing Wall.

Step	Foot Position and Direction	Turn	Footwork	Body Alignment
1.	Right foot to the side, a short step, against Line of Dance.	Nil.	Ball flat.	Facing Wall.
2.	Cross left foot behind right foot and check, against Line of Dance, in right side-by-side position.	¼ to left.	Ball flat.	Backing against Line of Dance.
3.	Replace weight forward to right foot, in place.	Turning to right.	Ball flat.	Facing Line of Dance.
4.	Left foot to the side, along Line of Dance.	¼ to right, over steps 3-4.	Ball flat.	Facing Wall.
5.	Close right foot towards left foot.	Nil.	Ball flat.	Facing Wall.
6.	Left foot to the side, a short step, along Line of Dance.	Nil.	Ball flat.	Facing Wall.
7.	Cross right foot behind left foot and check, down line of Dance, in left side-by-side position.	¼ to right.	Ball flat.	Backing Line of Dance.
8.	Replace weight forward to left foot, in place.	Turning to left.	Ball flat.	Facing against Line of Dance.

| 9. | **Right foot** to the side, against Line of Dance. | ¼ to left, over steps 3-4. | Ball flat. | Facing Wall. |
| 10. | Close **left foot** towards **right foot**. | Nil. | Ball flat. | Facing Wall. |

Rhythm: 1 – 2 – 3 – 4 – & – 1 – 2 – 3 – 4 – &
Calling Cues: Side – Cross – Rock – Cha – Cha – Side – Cross – Rock – Cha – Cha
Hold: On the preceding Cha Cha the man takes the lady's left hand in his right hand to end in Double Hold. The man releases the lady's right hand on step 2, retaining hold with his right hand to end in Right-Side-By-Side position. The man rejoins his left hand to lady's right hand on step 4 to end in Double Hold. The man releases the lady's left hand on step 7, retaining hold with his left hand to end in Left-Side-By-Side position. The man regains Close Hold position on step 10.

Lady's steps

Preparatory Position: Start facing Centre, weight on **right foot**, in Double Hold. End facing Centre.

Step	Foot Position and Direction	Turn	Footwork	Body Alignment
1.	**Left foot** to the side, a short step, against Line of Dance.	Nil.	Ball flat.	Facing Centre.
2.	Cross **right foot** behind **left foot** and check, against Line of Dance, in right side-by-side position.	¼ to right.	Ball flat.	Backing against Line of Dance
3.	Replace weight forward to **left foot**, in place.	Turning to left.	Ball flat.	Facing Line of Dance.
4.	**Right foot** to the side, along Line of Dance.	¼ to left, over steps 3-4.	Ball flat.	Facing Centre.
5.	Close **left foot** towards **right foot**.	Nil.	Ball flat.	Facing Centre.
6.	**Right foot** to the side, a short step, along Line of Dance.	Nil.	Ball flat.	Facing Centre.
7.	Cross **left foot** behind **right foot** and check, down Line of Dance, in left side-by-side position.	¼ to left.	Ball flat.	Backing Line of Dance.
8.	Replace weight forward to **right foot**, in place.	Turning to right.	Ball flat.	Facing against Line of Dance.

| 9. | **Left foot** to the side, against Line of Dance. | ¼ to right, over steps 3-4. | Ball flat. | Facing Centre. |
| 10. | Close **right foot** towards **left foot**. | Nil. | Ball flat. | Facing Centre. |

Rhythm: 1 – 2 – 3 – 4 – & – 1 – 2 – 3 – 4 – &
Calling Cues: Side – Cross – Rock – Cha – Cha – Side – Cross – Rock – Cha – Cha
Hold: On the preceding Cha Cha the lady joins her left hand to the man's right hand to end in Double Hold. The lady releases the right hand on step 2, retaining hold with her left hand to end in Right-Side-By-Side position. The lady rejoins her right hand on step 4 to end in Double Hold. The lady releases the left hand on step 7, retaining hold with right hand to end in Left-Side-By-Side position. The lady regains Close Hold position on step 10.

Your record collection can help to turn your kitchen into a dance studio! We've listed some of our favourite dance music on page 143.

Precedes and Follows

Right Foot Basic in Place
Before: Left Foot Basic in Place, Backward Basic Movement, Whisk to Left. Hand to Hand, Underarm Turn to Right and New Yorker.
After: Left Foot Basic in Place, Backward Basic Movement, Whisk to Left and Underarm Turn to Right.

Left Foot Basic in Place
Before: Right Foot Basic in Place, Forward Basic Movement and Whisk to Right.
After: Right Foot Basic in Place, Forward Basic Movement, Whisk to Right, New Yorker and Hand to Hand.

Underarm Turn to Right
Before: Right Foot Basic in Place, Forward Basic Movement and Whisk to Right.
After: Right Foot Basic in Place, Forward Basic Movement, Whisk to Right, New Yorker and Hand to Hand.

Forward Basic Movement
Before: Left Foot Basic in Place, Backward Basic Movement, Whisk to Left and Underarm Turn to Right.
After: Left Foot Basic in Place, Backward Basic Movement, Whisk to Left and Underarm Turn to Right.

Backward Basic Movement
Before: Right Foot Basic in Place, Forward Basic Movement and Whisk to Right.
After: Right Foot Basic in Place, Forward Basic Movement, Whisk to Right, New Yorker and Hand to Hand.

New Yorker
Before: Left Foot Basic in Place, Backward Basic Movement, Whisk to Left and Underarm Turn to Right.
After: Right Foot Basic in Place, Forward Basic Movement, Whisk to Right, New Yorker and Hand to Hand.

Whisk to Right
Before: Left Foot Basic in Place, Backward Basic Movement, Whisk to Left and Underarm Turn to Right.
After: Left Foot Basic in Place, Backward Basic Movement, Whisk to Left and Underarm Turn to Right.

Whisk to Left
Before: Right Foot Basic in Place, Forward Basic Movement and Whisk to Right.
After: Right Foot Basic in Place, Forward Basic Movement, Whisk to Right, New Yorker and Hand to Hand.

Hand to Hand

Before: Left Foot Basic in Place, Backward Basic Movement, Whisk to Left and Underarm Turn to Right.

After: Right Foot Basic in Place, Forward Basic Movement, Whisk to Right, New Yorker and Hand to Hand.

Practice Choreography

Routine One

Preparatory Position: Start facing Wall, weight on the **left foot**, in Close Hold. End facing Wall.

Right Foot Basic in Place. Left Foot Basic in Place. Right Foot Basic in Place. Underarm Turn to Right.

Routine Two

Preparatory Position: Start facing Wall, weight on the **left foot**, in Close Hold. End facing Wall.

Right Foot Basic in Place. Left Foot Basic in Place. Forward Basic Movement. Backward Basic Movement. Forward Basic Movement. Underarm Turn to Right.

Routine Three

Preparatory Position: Start facing Wall, weight on the **left foot**, in Close Hold. End facing Wall.

Forward Basic Movement. Backward Basic Movement. Forward Basic Movement. Underarm Turn to Right to end in Open Counter Promenade position. New Yorker. (Repeat New Yorker.)

Routine Four

Preparatory Position: Start facing Wall, weight on the **left foot**, in Close Hold. End facing Wall.

Whisk to Right. Whisk to Left. Whisk to Right. Whisk to Left. Steps 1 to 15 Hand to Hand. Underarm Turn to Right.

Routine Five

Preparatory Position: Start facing Wall, weight on the **left foot**, in Close Hold. End facing Wall.

Forward Basic Movement. Underarm Turn to Right (lady dances the turn while the man dances the Backward Basic Movement). End the turn in Open Counter Promenade position.

Steps 1 to 15 New Yorker. Man and lady release hold. Man dances the Left Foot Basic in Place, without hold, while the lady dances the Underarm Turn as a solo turn.

Salsa

Time signature: 4/4; four beats to the bar.

Rhythm: Each step takes one beat of music.

Tempo: A wide range, from slow to fast.

In recent years Salsa has soared in popularity in the UK. Visit one of the many Salsa clubs and you will quickly understand why. It is a relaxed, informal style of dance which shouldn't intimidate even novice dancers. So relax, enjoy the pace and get into the party mood. Although the foot pattern of the Salsa is the same as the Mambo, the Salsa is seen more as a solo dance at social occasions, with partners facing each other (known as the Challenge Position) or standing side-by-side. When dancing side-by-side the dancers start on the same foot. When in Challenge Position the opposite foot is used. Stronger emphasis of the rhythm is shown in the arms and body than that of a dance using Close Hold.

The use of the body alignment is written for learning purposes. When danced solo and using no progression, alignments are not necessary. I have charted the figures with the imaginary dancers in a Challenge Position, with the man facing the Wall and the lady facing Centre.

Action

Each step is taken with a slight hip swing, always in the direction in which the step is taken. When the tempo is fast more emphasis is placed on the foot speed and less on the body action.

New Position

Challenge Position

Man and lady stand facing each other at approximately arm's length, without hold. The arms are held at the side of the body with the arms bent with the forearms parallel to the floor.

Precedes and Follows and Practice Choreography

Dance the figures in the order they are written. This will give a full solo routine. Practise the figures also in a side-by-side position, both starting on the same foot, as an alternative routine.

Side Basic

Man's steps

Preparatory Position: Start facing Wall, weight on **right foot**, in Challenge Position. End facing Wall.

Step	Foot Position and Direction	Turn	Footwork	Body Alignment
1.	Tap **left foot**, in place.	No turn, throughout.	Ball.	Facing Wall, throughout.
2.	**Left foot** to the side, a short step, along Line of Dance.		Ball flat.	
3.	Close **right foot** to **left foot**.		Ball flat.	
4.	**Left foot** to the side, a short step, along Line of Dance.		Ball flat.	
5.	Tap **right foot** to **left foot**.		Ball.	
6.	**Right foot** to the side, a short step, against Line of Dance.		Ball flat.	
7.	Close **left foot** to **right foot**.		Ball flat.	
8.	**Right foot** to the side, a short step, against Line of Dance.		Ball flat.	

Rhythm: Quick – Quick – Quick – Quick – Quick – Quick – Quick – Quick
Calling Cues: Tap – Side – Close – Side – Tap – Side – Close – Side

Lady's steps

Preparatory Position: Start facing Centre, weight on **left foot**, in Challenge Position. End facing Centre.

Step	Foot Position and Direction	Turn	Footwork	Body Alignment
1.	Tap **right foot**, in place.	No turn, throughout.	Ball.	Facing Centre, throughout.
2.	**Right foot** to the side, a short step, along Line of Dance.		Ball flat.	

3.	Close **left foot** to **right foot**.	Ball flat.
4.	**Right foot** to the side, a short step, along Line of Dance.	Ball flat.
5.	Tap **left foot** to **right foot**.	Ball.
6.	**Left foot** to the side, a short step, against Line of Dance.	Ball flat.
7.	Close **right foot** to **left foot**.	Ball flat.
8.	**Left foot** to the side, a short step, against Line of Dance.	Ball flat.

Rhythm: Quick – Quick – Quick – Quick – Quick – Quick – Quick – Quick
Calling Cues: Tap – Side – Close – Side – Tap – Side – Close – Side

Cucaracha to Left

Man's steps

Preparatory Position: Start facing Wall, weight on **right foot**, in Challenge Position. End facing Wall.

Step	Foot Position and Direction	Turn	Footwork	Body Alignment
1.	Tap **left foot** to **right foot**.	No turn, throughout.	Ball.	Facing Wall, throughout.
2.	**Left foot** to the side, a short step, along Line of Dance.		Ball flat.	
3.	Replace weight to **right foot**.		Ball flat.	
4.	Close **left foot** to **right foot**.		Ball flat.	

Rhythm: Quick – Quick – Quick – Quick
Calling Cues: Tap – Side – Rock – Close

Lady's steps

Preparatory Position: Start facing Centre, weight on **left foot**, in Challenge Position. End facing Centre.

Step	Foot Position and Direction	Turn	Footwork	Body Alignment
1.	Tap **right foot** to **left foot**.	No turn, throughout.	Ball.	Facing Centre, throughout.
2.	**Right foot** to the side, a short step, along Line of Dance.		Ball flat.	
3.	Replace weight to **left foot**.		Ball flat.	
4.	Close **right foot** to **left foot**.		Ball flat.	

Rhythm: Quick – Quick – Quick – Quick
Calling Cues: Tap – Side – Rock – Close

Cucaracha to Right

Man's steps

Preparatory Position: Start facing Wall, weight on **left foot**, in Challenge Position. End facing Wall.

Step	Foot Position and Direction	Turn	Footwork	Body Alignment
1.	Tap **right foot** to **left foot**.	No turn, throughout.	Ball.	Facing Wall, throughout.
2.	**Right foot** to the side, a short step, against Line of Dance.		Ball flat.	
3.	Replace weight to **left foot**.		Ball flat.	
4.	Close **right foot** to **left foot**.		Ball flat.	

Rhythm: Quick – Quick – Quick – Quick
Calling Cues: Tap – Side – Rock – Close

Lady's steps

Preparatory Position: Start facing Centre, weight on **right foot**, in Challenge Position. End facing Centre.

Step	Foot Position and Direction	Turn	Footwork	Body Alignment
1.	Tap **left foot** to **right foot**.	No turn, throughout.	Ball.	Facing Centre, throughout.
2.	**Left foot** to the side, a short step, against Line of Dance.		Ball flat.	
3.	Replace weight to **right foot**.		Ball flat.	
4.	Close **left foot** to **right foot**.		Ball flat.	

Rhythm: Quick – Quick – Quick – Quick
Calling Cues: Tap – Side – Rock – Close

Forward Cucarachas

Man's steps

Preparatory Position: Start facing Wall, weight on **right foot**, in Challenge Position. End facing Wall.

Step	Foot Position and Direction	Turn	Footwork	Body Alignment
1.	Tap **left foot** to **right foot**.	No turn, throughout.	Ball.	Facing Wall, throughout.
2.	**Left foot** forward, to Wall.		Ball flat.	
3.	Replace weight back to **right foot**.		Ball flat.	
4.	Close **left foot** to **right foot**.		Ball flat.	
5.	Tap **right foot** to **left foot**.		Ball.	
6.	**Right foot** forward, to Wall.		Ball flat.	
7.	Replace weight back to **left foot**.		Ball flat.	
8.	Close **right foot** to **left foot**.		Ball flat.	

Rhythm: Quick – Quick – Quick – Quick – Quick – Quick – Quick – Quick
Calling Cues: Tap – Step – Rock – Close – Tap – Step – Rock – Close

Lady's steps

Preparatory Position: Start facing Centre, weight on **left foot**, in Challenge Position. End facing Centre.

Step	Foot Position and Direction	Turn	Footwork	Body Alignment
1.	Tap **right foot** to **left foot**.	No turn, throughout.	Ball.	Facing Centre, throughout.
2.	**Right foot** back, to Wall.		Ball flat.	
3.	Replace weight forward to **left foot**.		Ball flat.	
4.	Close **right foot** to **left foot**.		Ball flat.	
5.	Tap **left foot** to **right foot**.		Ball.	
6.	**Left foot** back, to Wall.		Ball flat.	
7.	Replace weight forward to **right foot**.		Ball flat.	
8.	Close **left foot** to **right foot**.		Ball flat.	

Rhythm: Quick – Quick – Quick – Quick – Quick – Quick – Quick – Quick
Calling Cues: Tap – Step – Rock – Close – Tap – Step – Rock – Close

Backward Cucarachas

Man's steps

Preparatory Position: Start facing Wall, weight on **right foot**, in Challenge Position. End facing Wall.

Step	Foot Position and Direction	Turn	Footwork	Body Alignment
1.	Tap **left foot** to **right foot**.	No turn, throughout.	Ball.	Facing Wall, throughout.
2.	**Left foot** back, to Centre.		Ball flat.	
3.	Replace weight forward to **right foot**.		Ball flat.	
4.	Close **left foot** to **right foot**.		Ball flat.	
5.	Tap **right foot** to **left foot**.		Ball.	

6.	**Right foot** back, to Centre.		Ball flat.	
7.	Replace weight forward to **left foot**.		Ball flat.	
8.	Close **right foot** to **left foot**.		Ball flat.	

Rhythm: Quick – Quick – Quick – Quick – Quick – Quick – Quick – Quick
Calling Cues: Tap – Step – Rock – Close – Tap – Step – Rock – Close

Lady's steps

Preparatory Position: Start facing Centre, weight on **left foot**, in Challenge Position. End facing Centre.

Step	Foot Position and Direction	Turn	Footwork	Body Alignment
1.	Tap **right foot** to **left foot**.	No turn, throughout.	Ball.	Facing Centre, throughout.
2.	**Right foot** forward, to Centre.		Ball flat.	
3.	Replace weight back to **left foot**.		Ball flat.	
4.	Close **right foot** to **left foot**.		Ball flat.	
5.	Tap **left foot** to **right foot**.		Ball.	
6.	**Left foot** forward, to Centre.		Ball flat.	
7.	Replace weight back to **right foot**.		Ball flat.	
8.	Close **left foot** to **right foot**.		Ball flat.	

Rhythm: Quick – Quick – Quick – Quick – Quick – Quick – Quick – Quick
Calling Cues: Tap – Step – Rock – Close – Tap – Step – Rock – Close

Mambo

Time signature: 4/4; four beats to the bar.

Rhythm: Each step takes one beat of music.

Tempo: A wide range from slow to fast.

The Mambo has been slow in gaining popularity in Europe, but since the dance has been featured in several films it has become accepted for any social programme. When first shown to the non-Latins, dancers found the music too fast and the rhythm too complicated. All this has long since past and today it is not unusual to hear a Mambo rhythm played in the popular music charts.

All the figures in the Salsa can be danced in the Mambo. When the Salsa figures are danced in the Mambo, Close Hold is used.

Action

Each step is taken with a slight hip swing, always in the direction in which the step is taken. When the tempo is fast more emphasis is placed on the foot speed and less on the body action. Quite often you will see the dancer replace the foot tap with a foot flick. That is, the stepping foot is flicked forward or backward from below the knee, with the foot slightly off the floor.

Mambo Basic

Man's steps

Preparatory Position: Start facing Wall, weight on **right foot**, in Close Hold. End facing Wall.

Step	Foot Position and Direction	Turn	Footwork	Body Alignment
1.	Tap **left foot** to **right foot**.	No turn, throughout.	Ball.	Facing Wall.
2.	**Left foot** forward, to Wall.		Ball flat.	Facing Wall.
3.	Replace weight back to **right foot**.		Ball flat.	Backing Centre.
4.	Close **left foot** to **right foot**.		Ball flat.	Backing Centre.
5.	Tap **right foot** to **left foot**.		Ball.	Backing Centre.
6.	**Right foot** back, to Centre.		Ball flat.	Backing Centre.
7.	Replace weight forward to **left foot**.		Ball flat.	Facing Wall.

| 8. | Close **right foot** to **left foot**. | | Ball flat. | Facing Wall. |

Rhythm: Quick – Quick – Quick – Quick – Quick – Quick – Quick – Quick
Calling Cues: Tap – Step – Rock – Close – Tap – Step – Rock – Close

Lady's steps

Preparatory Position: Start facing Centre, weight on **left foot**, in Close Hold.
End facing Centre.

Step	Foot Position and Direction	Turn	Footwork	Body Alignment
1.	Tap **right foot** to **left foot**.	No turn, throughout.	Ball.	Facing Centre.
2.	**Right foot** back, to Wall.		Ball flat.	Backing Wall.
3.	Replace weight forward to **left foot**.		Ball flat.	Facing Centre.
4.	Close **right foot** to **left foot**.		Ball flat.	Facing Centre.
5.	Tap **left foot** to **right foot**.		Ball.	Facing Centre.
6.	**Left foot** forward, to Centre.		Ball flat.	Facing Centre.
7.	Replace weight back to **right foot**.		Ball flat.	Backing Wall.
8.	Close **left foot** to **right foot**.		Ball flat.	Facing Centre.

Rhythm: Quick – Quick – Quick – Quick – Quick – Quick – Quick – Quick
Calling Cues: Tap – Step – Rock – Close – Tap – Step – Rock – Close

Check and Rocks in Open Promenade Position

Man's steps

Preparatory Position: Start facing Wall, weight on **right foot**, in Double Hold.
End facing Wall.

Step	Foot Position and Direction	Turn	Footwork	Body Alignment
1.	Tap **left foot** to **right foot**.	Nil.	Ball.	Facing Wall.
2.	**Left foot** to the side, a short step, along Line of Dance.	Body turn to left.	Ball flat.	Facing diagonally to Wall.

3.	**Right foot** forward and across **left foot** and check, in OPP.	$\frac{1}{4}$ to left, over steps 2-3.	Ball flat.	Facing Line of Dance.
4.	Replace weight back to **left foot**, in right side-by-side position.	Nil.	Ball flat.	Backing against Line of Dance.
5.	Replace weight forward to **right foot**, in OPP.	Nil.	Ball flat.	Facing Line of Dance.
6.	Replace weight back to **left foot**, in right side-by-side position.	Body turn to right.	Ball flat.	Backing against Line of Dance.
7.	**Right foot** to side, a short step, against Line of Dance, square to partner.	$\frac{1}{4}$ to right, over steps 6-7.	Ball flat.	Facing Wall.
8.	Replace weight to **Left foot**.	Nil.	Ball flat.	Facing Wall.

Rhythm: Quick – Quick – Quick – Quick – Quick – Quick – Quick – Quick
Calling Cues: Tap – Step – Check – Rock – Rock – Rock – Side – Rock
Hold: The man releases the lady's right hand on step 2, retaining hold of the lady's left hand. On step 7 he regains Close Hold or Double Hold.

Lady's steps

Preparatory Position: Start facing Centre, weight on **left foot**, in Close Hold. End facing Centre.

Step	Foot Position and Direction	Turn	Footwork	Body Alignment
1.	Tap **right foot** to **left foot**.	Nil.	Ball.	Facing Centre.
2.	**Right foot** to the side, a short step, along Line of Dance.	Body turn to right.	Ball flat.	Facing diagonally to Centre.
3.	**Left foot** forward and across **right foot** and check, in OPP.	$\frac{1}{4}$ to right over steps 2-3.	Ball flat.	Facing Line of Dance.
4.	Replace weight back to **right foot**, in right side-by-side position.	Nil.	Ball flat.	Backing against Line of Dance.
5.	Replace weight forward to **left foot** in OPP.	Nil.	Ball flat.	Facing Line of Dance.
6.	Replace weight back to **right foot**, in right side-by-side position.	Body turn to left.	Ball flat.	Backing against Line of Dance.

| 7. | **Left foot** to side, a short step, against Line of Dance, square to partner. | ¼ to left, over steps 6-7. | Ball flat. | Facing Centre. |
| 8. | Replace weight to **right foot**. | Nil. | Ball flat. | Facing Centre. |

Rhythm: Quick – Quick – Quick – Quick – Quick – Quick – Quick – Quick
Calling Cues: Tap – Step – Check – Rock – Rock – Rock – Side – Rock
Hold: The lady releases the right hand on step 2, retaining hold of the man's right hand. On step 7 regain Close Hold or Double Hold.

Check and Rocks in Open Counter Promenade Position
Man's steps

Preparatory Position: Start facing Wall, weight on **left foot**, in Double Hold. End facing Wall.

Step	Foot Position and Direction	Turn	Footwork	Body Alignment
1.	Tap **right foot** to **left foot**.	Nil.	Ball.	Facing Wall.
2.	**Right foot** to the side, a short step, against Line of Dance.	Body turn to right.	Ball flat.	Facing diagonally to Wall against Line of Dance.
3.	**Left foot** forward and across **right foot** and check, in OCPP.	¼ to right over steps 2-3.	Ball flat.	Facing against Line of Dance.
4.	Replace weight back to **right foot**, in left side-by-side position.	Nil.	Ball flat.	Backing Line of Dance.
5.	Replace weight forward to **left foot** in OCPP.	Nil.	Ball flat.	Facing against Line of Dance.
6.	Replace weight back to **right foot**, in left side-by-side position.	Body turn to left.	Ball flat.	Backing Line of Dance.
7.	**Left foot** to side, a short step, along Line of Dance, square to partner.	¼ to left, over steps 6-7.	Ball flat.	Facing Wall.
8.	Replace weight to **right foot**.	Nil.	Ball flat.	Facing Wall.

Rhythm: Quick – Quick – Quick – Quick – Quick – Quick – Quick – Quick
Calling Cues: Tap – Step – Check – Rock – Rock – Rock – Side – Rock
Hold: Release lady's left hand on step 2, retaining hold with left hand to lady's right hand. Rejoin to Double Hold or Close Hold on step 7.

Lady's steps

Preparatory Position: Start facing Centre, weight on **right foot**, in Double Hold. End facing Centre.

Step	Foot Position and Direction	Turn	Footwork	Body Alignment
1.	Tap **left foot** to **right foot**.	Nil.	Ball.	Facing Centre.
2.	**Left foot** to the side, a short step, against Line of Dance.	Body turn to left.	Ball flat.	Facing diagonally to Centre against Line of Dance.
3.	**Right foot** forward and across **left foot** and check, in OCPP.	¼ to left, over steps 2-3.	Ball flat.	Facing against Line of Dance.
4.	Replace weight back to **left foot**, in left side-by-side position.	Nil.	Ball flat.	Backing Line of Dance.
5.	Replace weight forward to **right foot**, in OCPP.	Nil.	Ball flat.	Facing against Line of Dance.
6.	Replace weight back to **left foot**, in left side-by-side position.	Body turn to right.	Ball flat.	Backing Line of Dance.
7.	**Right foot** to side, a short step, along Line of Dance, square to partner.	¼ to right, over steps 6-7.	Ball flat.	Facing Centre.
8.	Replace weight to **left foot**.	Nil.	Ball flat.	Facing Centre.

Rhythm: Quick – Quick – Quick – Quick – Quick – Quick – Quick – Quick
Calling Cues: Tap – Step – Check – Rock – Rock – Rock – Side – Rock
Hold: Release man's right hand on step 2, retaining hold with right hand to man's left hand. Rejoin to Double Hold or Close Hold on step 7.

The Underarm Turn to Right

Man's steps

Preparatory Position: Start facing Wall, weight on **right foot**, in Close Hold. End facing Wall.

Step	Foot Position and Direction	Turn	Footwork	Body Alignment
1.	Tap **left foot** to **right foot**.	No turn, throughout.	Ball.	Facing Wall.
2.	**Left foot** forward, to Wall.		Ball flat.	Facing Wall.
3.	Replace weight back to **right foot**.		Ball flat.	Backing Centre.
4.	**Left foot** to side, a short step, along Line of Dance.		Ball flat.	Backing Centre.
5.	Tap **right foot** to **left foot**.		Ball.	Backing Centre.
6.	**Right foot** back to Centre.		Ball flat.	Backing Centre.
7.	Replace weight forward to **left foot**.		Ball flat.	Facing Wall.
8.	Close **right foot** to **left foot**.		Ball flat.	Facing Wall.

Rhythm: Quick – Quick – Quick – Quick – Quick – Quick – Quick – Quick
Calling Cues: Tap – Step – Rock – Side – Tap – Step – Rock – Close
Hold: Raise the left hand on step 4, indicating with the right hand to the lady to turn under her raised right arm to the right, then release hold with the right hand. Rejoin to Close Hold on step 8.

Lady's steps

Preparatory Position: Start facing Centre, weight on **left foot**, in Close Hold. End facing Centre.

Step	Foot Position and Direction	Turn	Footwork	Body Alignment
1.	Tap **right foot** to **left foot**.	Nil.	Ball.	Facing Centre.
2.	**Right foot** back, to Wall.	Nil.	Ball flat.	Backing Wall.

3.	Replace weight forward to **left foot**.	Nil.	Ball flat.	Facing Centre.
4.	**Right foot** to side, a short step, along Line of Dance.	Body turn to right.	Ball flat.	Facing diagonally to Centre.
5.	Tap **left foot** to side.	Nil.	Ball.	Facing diagonally to Centre.
6.	**Left foot** forward, over **right foot**, down line of Dance.	Turning strongly to right.	Ball flat.	Facing Line of Dance.
7.	Replace weight forward to **Right foot**.	Continue to turn to right.	Ball flat.	Facing diagonally to Wall against Line of Dance.
8.	**Left foot** to side, a short step, against Line of Dance.	A complete turn to right, over steps 4-8.	Ball flat.	Facing Centre.

Rhythm: Quick – Quick – Quick – Quick – Quick – Quick – Quick – Quick
Calling Cues: Tap – Step – Rock – Side – Tap – Turn – Turn – Side
Hold: The right hand is raised on step 4. Releasing hold with the left hand, turn under the raised right arm to the right. Rejoin to Close Hold on step 8.

The Underarm Turn to Left

Man's steps

Preparatory Position: Start facing Wall, weight on **left foot**, in Close Hold. End facing Wall.

Step	Foot Position and Direction	Turn	Footwork	Body Alignment
1.	Tap **right foot** to **left foot**.	Nil.	Ball.	Facing Wall.
2.	**Right foot** back, to Centre.	Nil.	Ball flat.	Backing Centre.
3.	Replace weight forward to **left foot**.	Nil.	Ball flat.	Facing Wall.
4.	**Right foot** to side, a short step, against Line of Dance.	$\frac{1}{8}$ to right.	Ball flat.	Facing diagonally to Wall against Line of Dance.

5.	Tap **left foot** to side.	Nil.	Ball.	Facing diagonally to Wall against Line of Dance.
6.	**Left foot** forward, over **right foot**, diagonally to Wall against Line of Dance.	Nil.	Ball flat.	Facing diagonally to Wall against Line of Dance.
7.	Replace weight back to **Right foot**.	Turning to left.	Ball flat.	Backing diagonally to Centre.
8.	**Left foot** to side, along line of Dance.	⅛ to left, over steps 7-8.	Ball flat.	Facing Wall.

Rhythm: Quick – Quick – Quick – Quick – Quick – Quick – Quick – Quick
Calling Cues: Tap – Step – Rock – Side – Tap – Check – Rock – Side
Hold: Raise the left hand on step 4, indicating to the lady to turn to the left, then release hold with the right hand. Rejoin to Close Hold on step 8.

Lady's steps

Preparatory Position: Start facing Centre, weight on **right foot**, in Close Hold. End facing Centre.

Step	Foot Position and Direction	Turn	Footwork	Body Alignment
1.	Tap **left foot** to **right foot**.	Nil.	Ball.	Facing Centre.
2.	**Left foot** forward, to Centre.	Nil.	Ball flat.	Facing Centre.
3.	Replace weight back to **right foot**.	Nil.	Ball flat.	Backing Wall.
4.	**Left foot** to side, a short step, against Line of Dance.	⅛ to left.	Ball flat.	Facing diagonally to Centre against Line of Dance.
5.	Tap **right foot** to side.	Nil.	Ball.	Facing diagonally to Centre against Line of Dance.
6.	**Right foot** forward over **left foot**, against Line of Dance.	Turning to left.	Ball flat.	Facing against Line of Dance.

7.	Replace weight forward to **left foot**, down line of Dance.	Continue to turn	Ball flat.	Facing diagonally to Wall.
8.	**Right foot** to side, a short step, along Line of Dance.	A complete turn to left, over steps 4-8.	Ball flat.	Facing Centre.

Rhythm: Quick – Quick – Quick – Quick – Quick – Quick – Quick – Quick
Calling Cues: Tap – Step – Rock – Side – Tap – Turn – Turn – Side
Hold: The right hand is raised on step 4. Releasing hold with the left hand, turn under the raised right arm. Rejoin to Close Hold on step 8.

Precedes and Follows

Mambo Basic
Before: Mambo Basic, Check and Rocks in OCPP and Underarm Turn to Right.
After: Mambo Basic, Underarm Turn to Right and Check and Rocks in OPP.

Check and Rocks in Open Promenade Position
Before: Mambo Basic, Check and Rocks in OCPP and Underarm Turn to Right.
After: Mambo Basic, Check and Rocks in OCPP and Underarm Turn to Left.

Check and Rocks in Open Counter Promenade Position
Before: Check and Rocks in OPP and Underarm Turn to Left.
After: Mambo Basic, Check and Rocks in OPP and Underarm Turn to Right.

Underarm Turn to Right
Before: Mambo Basic, Check and Rocks in OCPP and Underarm Turn to Right.
After: Mambo Basic, Check and Rocks in OPP and Underarm Turn to Right.

Underarm Turn to Left
Before: Check and Rocks in OPP and Underarm Turn to Left.
After: Check and Rocks in OCPP and Underarm Turn to Left.

Practice Choreography

Routine One
Preparatory Position: Start facing Wall, weight on the **right foot**, in Close Hold. End facing Wall.
Dance the Mambo Basic, twice. Underarm Turn to Right.

Routine Two
Preparatory Position: Start facing Wall, weight on the **right foot**, in Close Hold. End facing Wall.
Dance the Mambo Basic, twice. Underarm Turn to Right. Check and Rocks in OPP.

Routine Three

Preparatory Position: Start facing Wall, weight on the **right foot**, in Close Hold. End facing Wall.

Dance the Mambo Basic, twice. Underarm Turn to Right. Check and Rocks in OPP. Check and Rocks in OCPP.

Routine Four

Preparatory Position: Start facing Wall, weight on the **right foot**, in Close Hold. End facing Wall.

Dance the Mambo Basic, twice. Underarm Turn to Right. Check and Rocks in OPP. Check and Rocks in OCPP. Dance 1-4 Mambo Basic. Underarm Turn to Left.

Routine Five (incorporating figures from the Salsa)

Preparatory Position: Start facing Wall, weight on the **right foot**, in Close Hold. End facing Wall.

Side Basic. Cucaracha to Left. Cucaracha to Right. Mambo Basic. Check and Rocks in OPP. Check and Rocks in OCPP. Underarm Turn to Right. Dance 1-4 Mambo Basic. Underarm Turn to Left.

Choose music with the right tempo and a strong rhthm when practising these Latin-American dances. There are some examples on page 143.

Rumba

Time signature: 4/4; four beats to the bar.

Rhythm: Slow = 2 beats, Quick = 1 beat.

Tempo: 28 bars per minute. (112mm.)

The Cuban Rumba – often called the classic dance of all the Latin dances – has been popular in its country of origin, Cuba, for over 400 years. Although the tempo (28 bars per minute, 112mm) is slower, the mood and figures still tell the story of the woman's attempt to lure the man into marriage by her sensuous actions. Figures from the Salsa, Mambo and Cha Cha Cha can be adapted to the Rumba figuration and rhythm.

Action

Each step is taken with a slight hip swing, always in the direction in which the step is taken.

Natural Square

Man's steps

Preparatory Position: Start facing Wall, weight on **left foot**, in Close Hold. End facing Wall.

Step	Foot Position and Direction	Turn	Footwork	Body Alignment
1.	**Right foot** forward, a short step, to Wall.	No turn, throughout.	Ball flat.	Facing Wall.
2.	**Left foot** to the side, along Line of Dance.		Ball flat.	Facing Wall.
3.	Close **right foot** to **left foot**.		Ball flat.	Facing Wall.
4.	**Left foot** back, a short step, to Centre.		Ball flat.	Backing Centre.
5.	**Right foot** to the side, against Line of Dance.		Ball flat.	Backing Centre.
6.	Close **left foot** to **right foot**.		Ball flat.	Facing Wall.

Rhythm: Quick – Quick – Slow – Quick – Quick – Slow
Calling Cues: Step – Side – Close – Step – Side – Close

Lady's steps

Preparatory Position: Start facing Centre, weight on **right foot**, in Close Hold.
End facing Centre.

Step	Foot Position and Direction	Turn	Footwork	Body Alignment
1.	**Left foot** back a short step, to Wall.	No turn, throughout.	Ball flat.	Backing Wall.
2.	**Right foot** to the side, along Line of Dance.		Ball flat.	Backing Wall.
3.	Close **left foot** to **right foot**.		Ball flat.	Backing Wall.
4.	**Right foot** forward, a short step, to Centre.		Ball flat.	Facing Centre.
5.	**Left foot** to the side, against Line of Dance.		Ball flat.	Facing Centre.
6.	Close **right foot** to **left foot**.		Ball flat.	Facing Centre.

Rhythm: Quick – Quick – Slow – Quick – Quick – Slow
Calling Cues: Step – Side – Close – Step – Side – Close

Reverse Square
Man's steps

Preparatory Position: Start facing Wall, weight on **right foot**, in Close Hold.
End facing Wall.

Step	Foot Position and Direction	Turn	Footwork	Body Alignment
1.	**Left foot** forward, a short step, to Wall.	No turn, throughout.	Ball flat.	Facing Wall.
2.	**Right foot** to the side, against Line of Dance.		Ball flat.	Facing Wall.
3.	Close **left foot** to **right foot**.		Ball flat.	Facing Wall.
4.	**Right foot** back, a short step, to Centre.		Ball flat.	Backing Centre.
5.	**Left foot** to the side, along Line of Dance.		Ball flat.	Backing Centre.
6.	Close **right foot** to **left foot**.		Ball flat.	Facing Wall.

Rhythm: Quick – Quick – Slow – Quick – Quick – Slow
Calling Cues: Step – Side – Close – Step – Side – Close

Lady's steps

Preparatory Position: Start facing Centre, weight on **left foot**, in Close Hold.
End facing Centre.

Step	Foot Position and Direction	Turn	Footwork	Body Alignment
1.	**Right foot** back a short step, to Wall.	No turn, throughout.	Ball flat.	Backing Wall.
2.	**Left foot** to the side, against Line of Dance.		Ball flat.	Backing Wall.
3.	Close **right foot** to **left foot**.		Ball flat.	Backing Wall.
4.	**Left foot** forward, a short step, to Centre.		Ball flat.	Facing Centre.
5.	**Right foot** to the side, along Line of Dance.		Ball flat.	Facing Centre.
6.	Close **left foot** to **right foot**.		Ball flat.	Facing Centre.

Rhythm: Quick – Quick – Slow – Quick – Quick – Slow
Calling Cues: Step – Side – Close – Step – Side – Close

Whisk to Right and Left

Man's steps

Preparatory Position: Start facing Wall, weight on **right foot**, in Close Hold.
End facing Wall.

Step	Foot Position and Direction	Turn	Footwork	Body Alignment
1.	Cross **left foot** behind **right foot**, in right side-by-side position.	¼ to left.	Ball flat.	Facing Line of Dance.
2.	Replace weight forward to **right foot**.	Body turn to right.	Ball flat.	Facing Line of Dance.
3.	**Left foot** to the side, along Line of Dance, square to partner.	¼ to right, over steps 2-3.	Ball flat.	Facing Wall.
4.	Cross **right foot** behind **left foot**, in left side-by-side position.	¼ to right.	Ball flat.	Facing against Line of Dance.
5.	Replace weight forward to **left foot**.	Body turn to left.	Ball flat.	Facing against Line of Dance.

| 6. | **Right foot** to side, against Line of Dance. | ¼ to left, over steps 5-6. | Ball flat. | Facing Wall. |

Rhythm: Quick – Quick – Slow – Quick – Quick – Slow
Calling Cues: Cross – Rock – Side – Cross – Rock – Side
Hold: Release hold with the left hand on step 1, retaining hold with the right hand. Place the left hand on the lady's back on step 3, releasing hold with the right hand. Regain Close Hold on step 6.

Lady's steps

Preparatory Position: Start facing Centre, weight on **left foot**, in Close Hold. End facing Centre.

Step	Foot Position and Direction	Turn	Footwork	Body Alignment
1.	Cross **right foot** behind **left foot**, in right side-by-side position.	¼ to right.	Ball flat.	Facing Line of Dance.
2.	Replace weight forward to **left foot**.	Body turn to left.	Ball flat.	Facing Line of Dance.
3.	**Right foot** to the side, along Line of Dance, square to partner.	¼ to left, over steps 2-3.	Ball flat.	Facing Centre.
4.	Cross **left foot** behind **right foot**, in left side-by-side position.	¼ to left.	Ball flat.	Facing against Line of Dance.
5.	Replace weight forward to **right foot**.	Body turn to right.	Ball flat.	Facing against Line of Dance.
6.	**Left foot** to side, against Line of Dance.	¼ to right, over steps 5-6.	Ball flat.	Facing Centre.

Rhythm: Quick – Quick – Slow – Quick – Quick – Slow
Calling Cues: Cross – Rock – Side – Cross – Rock – Side
Hold: Release hold with the right hand on step 1, retaining hold with the left hand. Place the right hand on the man's shoulder or his back on step 3, releasing hold with the left hand. Regain Close Hold on step 6.

Hand to Hand
Steps for man and lady
The figuration for the **Hand to Hand** is the same as the **Whisk to Right and Left**. The difference is seen in the hand holds:

✳ *Step 1 Man takes the lady's left hand in his right hand.*

✻ **Step 3** Man takes the lady's right hand into his left hand, retaining hold of the lady's left hand (Double Hold).

✻ **Step 4** Man releases lady's left hand, retaining hold of lady's right hand.

✻ *Step 6 Regain Close hold.*

Rhythm: Quick – Quick – Slow – Quick – Quick – Slow

Calling Cues: Cross – Rock – Side – Cross – Rock – Side

Basic Movement

Man's steps

Preparatory Position: Start facing Wall, weight on **right foot**, in Close Hold. End facing Wall.

Step	Foot Position and Direction	Turn	Footwork	Body Alignment
1.	**Left foot** forward, to Wall.	No turn, throughout.	Ball flat.	Facing Wall.
2.	Replace weight back to **right foot**.		Ball flat.	Backing Centre.
3.	**Left foot** to side, along Line of Dance.		Ball flat.	Backing Centre.
4.	**Right foot** back, to Centre.		Ball flat.	Backing Centre.
5.	Replace weight forward to **left foot**.		Ball flat.	Facing Wall.
6.	**Right foot** to side, against Line of Dance.		Ball flat.	Facing Wall.

Rhythm: Quick – Quick – Slow – Quick – Quick – Slow

Calling Cues: Step – Rock – Side – Step – Rock – Side

Lady's steps

Preparatory Position: Start facing Centre, weight on **left foot**, in Close Hold. End facing Centre.

Step	Foot Position and Direction	Turn	Footwork	Body Alignment
1.	**Right foot** back, to Wall.	No turn, throughout.	Ball flat.	Facing Centre.
2.	Replace weight forward to **left foot**.		Ball flat.	Facing Centre.
3.	**Right foot** to side, along Line of Dance.		Ball flat.	Facing Centre.
4.	**Left foot** forward, to Centre.		Ball flat.	Facing Centre.

| 5. | Replace weight back to **right foot**. | Ball flat. | Backing Wall. |
| 6. | **Left foot** to side, against Line of Dance. | Ball flat. | Facing Centre. |

Rhythm: Quick – Quick – Slow – Quick – Quick – Slow
Calling Cues: Step – Rock – Side – Step – Rock – Side

New Yorker

Man's steps

Preparatory Position: Start facing diagonally to Wall against Line of Dance, weight on **right foot**, in Open Counter Promenade position. End facing Wall.

Step	Foot Position and Direction	Turn	Footwork	Body Alignment
1.	**Left foot** forward, over **right foot** and check, against Line of Dance, in OCPP.	⅛ to right.	Ball flat.	Facing against Line of Dance.
2.	Replace weight back to **right foot**, in place.	Body turn to left.	Ball flat.	Backing Line of Dance.
3.	**Left foot** to the side, a short step, along line of Dance, in OPP.	⅜ to left, over steps 2-4.	Ball flat.	Facing diagonally to Wall.
4.	**Right foot** forward, over **left foot** and check, down line of Dance.	⅛ to left.	Ball flat.	Facing Line of Dance.
5.	Replace weight back to **left foot**, in place.	Body turn to right.	Ball flat.	Backing against Line of Dance.
6.	**Right foot** to the side, against Line of Dance.	¼ to right, over steps 5-6.	Ball flat.	Facing Wall.

Rhythm: Quick – Quick – Slow – Quick – Quick – Slow
Calling Cues: Check – Rock – Side – Check – Rock – Side
Hold: Release hold with the right hand on step 1, retaining hold with the left hand. Rejoin the right hand to lady's left hand on step 3 (Double Hold). Release hold with the left hand on step 4, retaining hold with the right hand. Rejoin to Close Hold on step 6.

Lady's steps

Preparatory Position: Start facing diagonally to Centre against Line of Dance, weight on **left foot**, in Open Counter Promenade position. End facing Centre.

Step	Foot Position and Direction	Turn	Footwork	Body Alignment
1.	**Right foot** forward, over **left foot** and check, against Line of Dance, in OCPP.	$\frac{1}{8}$ to left.	Ball flat.	Facing against Line of Dance.
2.	Replace weight back to **left foot**, in place.	Body turn to right.	Ball flat.	Backing Line of Dance.
3.	**Right foot** to the side, a short step, along line of Dance, in OPP.	$\frac{3}{8}$ to right, over steps 2-4.	Ball flat.	Facing diagonally to Centre.
4.	**Left foot** forward, over **right foot** and check, down line of Dance, in OPP.	$\frac{1}{8}$ to right.	Ball flat.	Facing Line of Dance.
5.	Replace weight back to **right foot**, in place.	Body turn to left.	Ball flat.	Backing against Line of Dance.
6.	**Left foot** to the side, against Line of Dance.	$\frac{1}{4}$ to left, over steps 5-6.	Ball flat.	Facing Centre.

Rhythm: Quick – Quick – Slow – Quick – Quick – Slow
Calling Cues: Check – Rock – Side – Check – Rock – Side
Hold: Release hold with the left hand on step 1, retaining hold with the right hand. Rejoin the left hand to man's right hand on step 3 (Double Hold). Release hold with the right hand on step 4, retaining hold with the left hand. Rejoin to Close Hold on step 6.

Precedes and Follows

Natural Square
Before: Natural Square and 1-3 Reverse Square.
After: Natural Square and 4-6 Reverse Square.

Reverse Square
Before: Reverse Square, 1-3 Natural Square, Basic Movement, Whisk to Right and Left, Hand to Hand and New Yorker.
After: Reverse Square, 4-6 Natural Square, Basic Movement, Whisk to Right and Left and Hand to Hand.

Whisk to Right and Left
Before: Whisk to Right and Left, Reverse Square, Hand to Hand, Basic Movement and New Yorker.

After: Whisk to Right and Left, Hand to Hand, Basic Movement and New Yorker.

Hand to Hand

Before: Hand to Hand, Whisk to Right and Left, Basic Movement, Reverse Square and New Yorker.

After: Hand to Hand, Whisk to Right and Left, Basic Movement, Reverse Square and New Yorker.

Basic Movement

Before: Basic Movement, Reverse Square, New Yorker, Hand to Hand and Whisk to Right and Left.

After: Basic Movement, Reverse Square, New Yorker, Hand to Hand and Whisk to Right and Left.

New Yorker

Before: Basic Movement, New Yorker, Hand to Hand and Whisk to Right and Left.

After: Basic Movement, Reverse Square, New Yorker, Hand to Hand and Whisk to Right and Left.

Practice Choreography

Routine One

Preparatory Position: Start facing Wall, weight on the **left foot**, in Close Hold. End facing Wall.

Natural Square. 1-3 Natural Square. Reverse Square. 1-3 Reverse Square.

Routine Two

Preparatory Position: Start facing Wall, weight on the **right foot**, in Close Hold. End facing Wall.

Reverse Square. Basic Movement. Reverse Square. Basic Movement.

Routine Three

Preparatory Position: Start facing Wall, weight on the **right foot**, in Close Hold. End facing Wall.

Basic Movement, end in OCPP. Dance New Yorker, twice.

Routine Four

Preparatory Position: Start facing Wall, weight on the **right foot**, in Close Hold. End facing Wall.

Basic Movement, end in OCPP. Dance New Yorker. Whisk to Right and Left.

Routine Five

Preparatory Position: Start facing Wall, weight on the **right foot**, in Close Hold. End facing Wall.

Basic Movement. Hand to Hand, twice. New Yorker, twice.

Samba

Time signature: 2/4; two beats to the bar.

Rhythm: Slow = 1 beat, Quick = ½ beat. (Advanced dancers use a rhythm of 1, a2. Step 1 — ¾ beat. Step 2 — ¼ beat. Step 3. 1 beat. This means that when closing the foot on steps 2 and 4, a quick weight change takes place for the count of 'a', before placing the weight to the other foot for the count of '2'.)

Tempo: 56 bars per minute. (112mm.)

The Samba is the national dance of Brazil. Many of the figures danced in its original form are still danced today in the social style of the Samba. Unlike some of our previous Latin dances, the Samba is a progressive dance that moves in an anti-clockwise direction around the room. There is a characteristic action called the bounce action, that the social dancer should try to master to get the full enjoyment from this dance. Practise the bounce action and then incorporate the bounce into the figures.

The Bounce Action

Preparatory Position: Commence with the feet together, both knees slightly flexed with the body weight on the **left foot**.

❉ **Right foot** forward, straightening the knees then flex the knees as weight is taken on to the **right foot**.

❉ Close **left foot** towards **right foot**, without weight, straightening the knees then flex the knees as **left foot** is closed to **right foot**.

❉ **Left foot** back, straightening the knees then flex the knees as weight is taken on to the **left foot**.

❉ Close **right foot** towards **left foot**, without weight, straightening the knees then flex the knees as **right foot** is closed to **left foot**.

Natural Basic Movement

Man's steps

Preparatory Position: Start facing Line of Dance, weight on **left foot**, in Close Hold. End facing Line of Dance.

Step	Foot Position and Direction	Turn	Footwork	Body Alignment
1.	**Right foot** forward, down line of Dance.	No turn, throughout.	Ball flat.	Facing Line of Dance.
2.	Close **left foot** to **right foot**, without weight.		Ball.	Facing Line of Dance.

Step	Foot Position and Direction	Turn	Footwork	Body Alignment
3.	**Left foot** back, against Line of Dance.		Ball flat.	Backing Line of Dance.
4.	Close **right foot** to **left foot**, without weight.		Ball.	Facing Line of Dance.

Rhythm: Slow – Slow – Slow – Slow
Calling Cues: Step – Tap – Step – Tap

Lady's steps

Preparatory Position: Start backing Line of Dance, weight on **right foot**, in Close Hold. End backing Line of Dance.

Step	Foot Position and Direction	Turn	Footwork	Body Alignment
1.	**Left foot** back, down line of Dance.	No turn, throughout.	Ball flat.	Backing Line of Dance.
2.	Close **right foot** to **left foot**, without weight.		Ball.	Backing Line of Dance.
3.	**Right foot** forward, against Line of Dance.		Ball flat.	Facing against Line of Dance.
4.	Close **left foot** to **right foot**, without weight.		Ball.	Backing Line of Dance.

Rhythm: Slow – Slow – Slow – Slow
Calling Cues: Step – Tap – Step – Tap

Reverse Basic Movement

Man's steps

Preparatory Position: Start facing Line of Dance, weight on **right foot**, in Close Hold. End facing Line of Dance.

Step	Foot Position and Direction	Turn	Footwork	Body Alignment
1.	**Left foot** forward, down line of Dance.	No turn, throughout.	Ball flat.	Facing Line of Dance.
2.	Close **right foot** to **left foot**, without weight.		Ball.	Facing Line of Dance.
3.	**Right foot** back, against Line of Dance.		Ball flat.	Backing against Line of Dance.
4.	Close **left foot** to **right foot**, without weight.		Ball.	Facing Line of Dance.

Rhythm: Slow – Slow – Slow – Slow
Calling Cues: Step – Tap – Step – Tap

Lady's steps

Preparatory Position: Start backing Line of Dance, weight on **left foot**, in Close Hold. End backing Line of Dance.

Step	Foot Position and Direction	Turn	Footwork	Body Alignment
1.	**Right foot** back, down line of Dance.	No turn, throughout.	Ball flat.	Backing Line of Dance.
2.	Close **left foot** to **right foot**, without weight.		Ball.	Backing Line of Dance.
3.	**Left foot** forward, against Line of Dance.		Ball flat.	Facing against Line of Dance.
4.	Close **right foot** to **left foot**, without weight.		Ball.	Backing Line of Dance.

Rhythm: Slow – Slow – Slow – Slow
Calling Cues: Step – Tap – Step – Tap

Side Step to Right and Left

Man's steps

Preparatory Position: Start facing Line of Dance, weight on **left foot**, in Close Hold. End facing Line of Dance.

Step	Foot Position and Direction	Turn	Footwork	Body Alignment
1.	**Right foot** to side, to Wall.	No turn, throughout.	Ball flat.	Facing Line of Dance, throughout.
2.	Close **left foot** to **right foot**, without weight.		Ball.	
3.	**Left foot** to side, to Centre.		Ball flat.	
4.	Close **right foot** to **left foot**, without weight.		Ball.	

Rhythm: Slow – Slow – Slow – Slow
Calling Cues: Side – Tap – Side – Tap

Lady's steps

Preparatory Position: Start backing Line of Dance, weight on **right foot**, in Close Hold. End backing Line of Dance.

Step	Foot Position and Direction	Turn	Footwork	Body Alignment
1.	**Left foot** to side, to Wall.	No turn, throughout.	Ball flat.	Backing Line of Dance, throughout.
2.	Close **right foot** to **left foot**, without weight.		Ball.	
3.	**Right foot** to side, to Centre.		Ball flat.	
4.	Close **left foot** to **right foot**, without weight.		Ball.	

Rhythm: Slow – Slow – Slow – Slow
Calling Cues: Side – Tap – Side – Tap

Progressive Basic

Man's steps

Preparatory Position: Start facing diagonally to Wall, weight on **left foot**, in Close Hold. End facing diagonally to Wall.

Step	Foot Position and Direction	Turn	Footwork	Body Alignment
1.	**Right foot** forward, diagonally to Wall.	No turn, throughout.	Ball flat.	Facing diagonally to Wall, throughout.
2.	Close **left foot** to **right foot**, without weight.		Ball.	
3.	**Left foot** to side, diagonally to Centre.		Ball flat.	
4.	Close **right foot** to **left foot**, without weight.		Ball.	

Rhythm: Slow – Slow – Slow – Slow
Calling Cues: Step – Tap – Side – Tap
Note: Facing diagonally to Wall when dancing the Progressive Basic ensures that steps 2 and 4 progress along the side of the room. It could be danced facing Line of Dance.

Lady's steps

Preparatory Position: Start backing diagonally to Wall, weight on **right foot**, in Close Hold. End backing diagonally to Wall.

Step	Foot Position and Direction	Turn	Footwork	Body Alignment
1.	**Left foot** back, diagonally to Wall.	No turn, throughout.	Ball flat.	Backing diagonally to Wall, throughout.
2.	Close **right foot** to **left foot**, without weight.		Ball.	
3.	**Right foot** to side, diagonally to Centre.		Ball flat.	
4.	Close **left foot** to **right foot**, without weight.		Ball.	

Rhythm: Slow – Slow – Slow – Slow
Calling Cues: Step – Tap – Side – Tap
Note: Backing diagonally to Wall when dancing the Progressive Basic ensures that steps 2 and 4 progress along the side of the room. It could be danced, as the lady, backing Line of Dance.

Outside Basic

Man's steps

Preparatory Position: Start facing Line of Dance, weight on **left foot**, in Close Hold. End facing Line of Dance.

Step	Foot Position and Direction	Turn	Footwork	Body Alignment
1.	**Right foot** forward, down line of Dance.	Nil.	Ball flat.	Facing Line of Dance.
2.	Close **left foot** to **right foot**, without weight.	$\frac{1}{8}$ to left.	Ball.	Backing diagonally to Wall against Line of Dance
3.	**Left foot** back, diagonally to Wall against Line of Dance, partner outside.	Nil.	Ball flat.	Backing diagonally to Wall against Line of Dance.
4.	Close **right foot** to **left foot**, without weight.	Nil.	Ball.	Facing diagonally to Centre.

5.	**Right foot** forward, diagonally to Centre, outsde partner.	Nil.	Ball flat.	Facing diagonally to Centre.
6.	Close **left foot** to **right foot**, without weight.	⅛ to right.	Ball.	Backing against Line of Dance.
7.	**Left foot** back, against Line of Dance.	Nil.	Ball flat.	Backing against Line of Dance.
8.	Close **right foot** to **left foot**, without weight.	Nil.	Ball.	Facing Line of Dance.

Rhythm: Slow – Slow – Slow – Slow – Slow – Slow – Slow – Slow
Calling Cues: Step – Turn – Step – Tap – Step – Turn – Step – Tap

Lady's steps

Preparatory Position: Start backing Line of Dance, weight on **right foot**, in Close Hold. End backing Line of Dance.

Step	Foot Position and Direction	Turn	Footwork	Body Alignment
1.	**Left foot** back, down line of Dance.	Nil.	Ball flat.	Backing Line of Dance.
2.	Close **right foot** to **left foot**, without weight.	⅛ to left.	Ball.	Facing diagonally to Wall against Line of Dance.
3.	**Right foot** forward, diagonally to Wall against Line of Dance, outside partner.	Nil.	Ball flat.	Facing diagonally to Wall against Line of Dance.
4.	Close **left foot** to **right foot**, without weight.	Nil.	Ball.	Backing diagonally to Centre.
5.	**Left foot** back, diagonally to Centre, partner outside.	Nil.	Ball flat.	Backing diagonally to Centre.
6.	Close **right foot** to **left foot**, without weight.	⅛ to right.	Ball.	Facing against Line of Dance.
7.	**Right foot** forward, against Line of Dance.	Nil.	Ball flat.	Facing against Line of Dance.
8.	Close **left foot** to **right foot**, without weight.	Nil.	Ball.	Backing Line of Dance.

Rhythm: Slow – Slow – Slow – Slow – Slow – Slow – Slow – Slow
Calling Cues: Step – Turn – Step – Tap – Step – Turn – Step – Tap

Chassé Walks on Right Foot and Left Foot
Man's steps

Preparatory Position: Start facing Line of Dance, weight on **left foot**, in Close Hold. End facing Line of Dance.

Step	Foot Position and Direction	Turn	Footwork	Body Alignment
1.	**Right foot** forward, a short step, down Line of Dance.	No turn, or a gradual turn to the right or left, making a ¼ turn over steps 1-6.	Ball flat.	Facing Line of Dance, throughout.
2.	Close **left foot** towards **right foot**.		Ball.	
3.	**Right foot** forward, a short step, down line of Dance.		Ball flat.	
4.	**Left foot** forward, a short step, down line of Dance.		Ball flat.	
5.	Close **right foot** towards **left foot**.		Ball.	
6.	**Left foot** forward, a short step, down line of Dance.		Ball flat.	

Rhythm: Slow – Quick – Quick – Slow – Quick – Quick
Calling Cues: Step – Close – Step – Step – Close – Step
Note: The Walks can be danced in Promenade position and also commenced starting with the **left foot**. Can also be danced without hold.

Lady's steps

Preparatory Position: Start backing Line of Dance, weight on **right foot**, in Close Hold. End backing Line of Dance.

Step	Foot Position and Direction	Turn	Footwork	Body Alignment
1.	**Left foot** back, a short step, down line of Dance.	No turn, or a gradual turn to the right or left, making a ¼ turn over steps 1-6.	Ball flat.	Backing Line of Dance, throughout.
2.	Close **right foot** towards **left foot**.		Ball.	
3.	**Left foot** back, a short step, down line of Dance.		Ball flat.	
4.	**Right foot** back, a short step, down line of Dance.		Ball flat.	
5.	Close **left foot** towards **right foot**.		Ball.	
6.	**Right foot** back, a short step, down line of Dance.		Ball flat.	

Rhythm: Slow – Quick – Quick – Slow – Quick -Quick
Calling Cues: Step – Close – Step – Step – Close – Step
Note: The Walks can be danced in Promenade position and also commenced starting with the **right foot**.

Whisk to Right and Left

Man's steps
Preparatory Position: Start facing Line of Dance, weight on **left foot**, in Close Hold. End facing Line of Dance.

Step	Foot Position and Direction	Turn	Footwork	Body Alignment
1.	**Right foot** to side, to Wall.	No turn, throughout.	Ball flat.	Facing Line of Dance, throughout.
2.	Close **left foot** to right heel, **left foot** turned slightly out.		Ball.	

3.	Replace weight to **right foot**, in place.	Ball flat.
4.	**Left foot** to side, to Centre.	Ball flat.
5.	Close **right foot** to left heel, **right foot** turned slightly out.	Ball.
6.	Replace weight to **left foot**, in place.	Ball flat.

Rhythm: Slow – Quick – Quick – Slow – Quick – Quick
Calling Cues: Side – Cross – Step – Side – Cross – Step
Note: The Whisk to Right can end in Promenade position.

Lady's steps

Preparatory Position: Start backing Line of Dance, weight on **right foot**, in Close Hold. End backing Line of Dance.

Step	Foot Position and Direction	Turn	Footwork	Body Alignment
1.	**Left foot** to side, to Wall.	No turn, throughout.	Ball flat.	Backing Line of Dance, throughout.
2.	Close **right foot** to left heel, **right foot** turned slightly out.		Ball.	
3.	Replace weight to **left foot**, in place.		Ball flat.	
4.	**Right foot** to side, to Centre.		Ball flat.	
5.	Close **left foot** to right heel, **left foot** turned slightly out.		Ball.	
6.	Replace weight to **right foot**, in place.		Ball flat.	

Rhythm: Slow – Quick – Quick – Slow – Quick – Quick
Calling Cues: Side – Cross – Step – Side – Cross – Step

Precedes and Follows

Natural Basic Movement

Before: Natural Basic Movement, Side Step to Right and Left, Progressive Basic, Outside Basic, Chassé Walks on Right Foot and Left Foot and Whisk to Right and Left.

After: Natural Basic Movement, Side Step to Right and Left, Progressive Basic, Outside Basic, Chassé Walks on Right Foot and Left Foot and Whisk to Right and Left.

Reverse Basic

Before: Reverse Basic, 1-2 Natural Basic, Whisk to Right and Side Step to Right.

After: Reverse Basic, Whisk to Left and Side Step to Left.

Side Step to Right and Left

Before: Natural Basic Movement, Side Step to Right and Left, Progressive Basic, Outside Basic, Chassé Walks on Right Foot and Left Foot and Whisk to Right and Left.

After: Natural Basic Movement, Side Step to Right and Left, Progressive Basic, Outside Basic, Chassé Walks on Right Foot and Left Foot and Whisk to Right and Left.

Progressive Basic

Before: Natural Basic Movement, Side Step to Right and Left, Progressive Basic, Outside Basic, Chassé Walks on Right Foot and Left Foot and Whisk to Right and Left.

After: Natural Basic Movement, Side Step to Right and Left, Progressive Basic, Outside Basic, Chassé Walks on Right Foot and Left Foot and Whisk to Right and Left.

Chassé Walks on Right Foot and Left Foot

Before: Natural Basic Movement, Side Step to Right and Left, Progressive Basic, Outside Basic, Chassé Walks on Right Foot and Left Foot and Whisk to Right and Left.

After: Natural Basic Movement, Side Step to Right and Left, Progressive Basic, Outside Basic, Chassé Walks on Right Foot and Left Foot and Whisk to Right and Left.

Whisk to Right and Left

Before: Natural Basic Movement, Side Step to Right and Left, Progressive Basic, Outside Basic, Chassé Walks on Right Foot and Left Foot and Whisk to Right and Left.

After: Natural Basic Movement, Side Step to Right and Left, Progressive Basic, Outside Basic, Chassé Walks on Right Foot and Left Foot and Whisk to Right and Left.

Practice Choreography

Routine One

Preparatory Position: Start facing Line of Dance, weight on the **left foot**, in Close Hold. End facing Line of Dance.
Natural Basic Movement. 1-2 Natural Basic Movement. Reverse Basic Movement. 1-2 Reverse Basic Movement.

Routine Two

Preparatory Position: Start facing Line of Dance, weight on the **left foot**, in Close Hold. End facing diagonally to Wall.
Natural Basic Movement, end facing diagonally to Wall. Dance the Progressive Basic, twice.

Routine Three

Preparatory Position: Start facing Line of Dance, weight on the **left foot**, in Close Hold. End facing Line of Dance.
Natural Basic Movement. Whisks to Right and Left. Progressive Basic.

Routine Four

Preparatory Position: Start facing Line of Dance, weight on the **left foot**, in Close Hold. End facing Line of Dance.
Natural Basic. Chassé Walks on Right Foot and Left Foot, twice. Outside Basic.

Routine Five

Preparatory Position: Start facing Wall, weight on the **left foot**, in Close Hold. End facing Line of Dance.
Side Step Right and Left. Whisk to Right, Left and Right to end in Promenade position. Chassé Walks on Left Foot and Right Foot, twice, in Promenade position. Turning to right, Whisk to Left, turning lady square, to end facing Wall. 1-2 Natural Basic Movement. 1-6. Reverse Basic Movement, to end facing diagonally to Wall. Progressive Basic, twice.1-2 Natural Basic Movement. 1-2 Reverse Basic Movement, to end facing Line of Dance.

Dances for Discos

Nice as it is to dance Ballroom and Latin, the fact is that many social occasions only have a discotheque or sometimes a live band playing chart music. Dance floors at these events are often small and crowded, but this doesn't mean that you have to jig about on your own like everybody else. In this section, we show you how to look good even in a crowded venue, dancing to the latest music!

Note: French-style Rock and Roll (also known as Modern Jive or Le Roc) is not covered in this book due to lack of space. Sigma Leisure do, however, publish a separate book and CD package ('Learn to Dance Modern Jive') and a full-length CD and booklet ('Start to Dance Modern Jive'). Details are at the back of this book.

Everybody will have some suitable music to practise these dances – but start with slow ones first!

Night Club Swing

Time signature: 4/4; four beats to the bar.

Rhythm: Each step takes one beat of music.

Tempo: Virtually any speed, from slow to fast.

Undoubtedly the Night Club Swing developed from the Hustle – a dance that was popular in the 70s and 80s. It makes a refreshing change from solo disco dancing to be able to have contact with a partner whilst still dancing to the latest record releases.

The Hold

Partners face each other in Double Hold, approximately one arm's length away. The joined hands are held in front of the bodies, approximately hip high. The construction of the dance is built on circular walks, this means the man and lady dance in their own space, interchanging in this space during the dance.

Action

The body action is more pronounced with the slower tempo. With each transference of weight the man and lady allow the hips to swing softly to the side. When the weight is transferred to the **left foot**, allow the hip to swing softly to the **left**. Transfer the weight to **right foot**, and the hip swings softly to the **right**.

Precedes and Follows and Practice Choreography

Dance the figures in the order they are written. This will give a full routine.

Basic Swing Step

Man's steps

Preparatory Position: Start facing Wall, weight on **right foot**, in Double Hold. End facing Wall.

Step	Foot Position and Direction	Turn	Footwork	Body Alignment
1.	Tap **left foot** to side, along Line of Dance.	No turn, throughout.	Ball.	Facing Wall.
2.	Almost close **left foot** to **right foot**.		Ball flat.	Facing Wall.
3.	Tap **right foot** to side, against Line of Dance.		Ball.	Facing Wall.
4.	Almost close **right foot** to **left foot**.		Ball flat.	Facing Wall.

5.	**Left foot** back, to Centre.	Ball flat.	Backing Centre.
6.	Replace weight forward to **right foot**, in place.	Ball flat.	Facing Wall.

Rhythm: 1 – 2 – 3 – 4 – 5 – 6
Calling Cues: Tap – Step – Tap – Step – Push – Pull
Hold: On step 5 the man extends the arms forward, leading the lady to step back. On step 6 he retracts the arms slightly, leading the lady to replace her weight forward.

Lady's steps

Preparatory Position: Start facing Centre, weight on **left foot**, in Double Hold. End facing Centre.

Step	Foot Position and Direction	Turn	Footwork	Body Alignment
1.	Tap **right foot** to side, along Line of Dance.	No turn, throughout.	Ball.	Facing Centre.
2.	Almost close **right foot** to **left foot**.		Ball flat.	Facing Centre.
3.	Tap **left foot** to side, against Line of Dance.		Ball.	Facing Centre.
4.	Almost close **left foot** to **right foot**.		Ball flat.	Facing Centre.
5.	**Right foot** back, to Wall.		Ball flat.	Backing Wall.
6.	Replace weight forward to **left foot**, in place.		Ball flat.	Facing Centre.

Rhythm: 1 – 2 – 3 – 4 – 5 – 6
Calling Cues: Tap – Step – Tap – Step – Push – Pull
Hold: The lady keeps the arms in tension to allow the man to lead her to step back on step 5, then to replace her weight forward on step 6.

Breakaway

Man's steps

Preparatory Position: Start facing Wall, weight on **right foot**, in Double Hold. End facing Wall.

Step	Foot Position and Direction	Turn	Footwork	Body Alignment
1.	Tap **left foot** to side, along Line of Dance.	Nil.	Ball.	Facing Wall.
2.	Almost close **left foot** to **right foot**.	Nil.	Ball flat.	Facing Wall.

3.	Tap **right foot** to side, against Line of Dance.	Nil.	Ball.	Facing Wall.
4.	**Right foot** back, to Centre.	⅛ to right.	Ball flat.	Backing diagonally to Centre.
5.	Close **left foot** to **right foot**.	Nil.	Ball flat.	Facing diagonally to Wall against Line of Dance.
6.	**Right foot** forward, to Wall.	⅛ to left.	Heel flat.	Facing Wall.

Rhythm: 1 – 2 – 3 – 4 – 5 – 6
Calling Cues: Tap – Step – Tap – Break – Close – Step
Hold: Release hold with the right hand on step 4. On step 5 raise the right hand above the head, the arm vertical. Rejoin to Double Hold on step 6.

Lady's steps

Preparatory Position: Start facing Centre, weight on **left foot**, in Double Hold. End facing Centre.

Step	Foot Position and Direction	Turn	Footwork	Body Alignment
1.	Tap **right foot** to side, along Line of Dance.	Nil.	Ball.	Facing Centre
2.	Almost close **right foot** to **left foot**.	Nil.	Ball flat.	Facing Centre.
3.	Tap **left foot** to side, against Line of Dance.	Nil.	Ball.	Facing Centre.
4.	**Left foot** back, to Wall.	⅛ turn to left.	Ball flat.	Facing diagonally to Centre against Line of Dance.
5.	Close **right foot** to **left foot**.	Nil.	Ball flat.	Facing diagonally to Centre against Line of Dance.
6.	**Left foot** forward, to Centre.	⅛ turn to right.	Heel flat.	Facing Centre.

Rhythm: 1 – 2 – 3 – 4 – 5 – 6
Calling Cues: Tap – Step – Tap – Break – Close – Step
Hold: Release hold with the left hand on step 4. On step 5 raise the left hand above the head, the arm vertical. Rejoin to Double Hold on step 6.

The Pass

Man's steps

Preparatory Position: Start facing Wall, weight on **right foot**, in Double Hold. End facing Centre.

Step	Foot Position and Direction	Turn	Footwork	Body Alignment
1.	Tap **left foot** to side, along Line of Dance.	Nil.	Ball.	Facing Wall.
2.	Almost close **left foot** to **right foot**.	Nil.	Ball flat.	Facing Wall.
3.	Tap **right foot** to side, against Line of Dance.	Nil.	Ball.	Facing Wall.
4.	**Right foot** forward, to Wall.	Turning to right.	Heel flat.	Facing Wall.
5.	**Left foot** forward, diagonally to Wall against Line of Dance.	Continue to turn.	Heel flat.	Facing diagonally to Wall against Line of Dance.
6.	Close **right foot** to left foot.	½ to right, over steps 4 – 6.	Ball flat.	Facing Centre.

Rhythm: 1 – 2 – 3 – 4 – 5 – 6
Calling Cues: Tap – Step – Tap – Walk – Turn – Close
Hold: Steps 4 – 5, arms are extended to the sides, parallel to the floor. Lower the arms on step 6. Over Steps 4 – 5, man and lady place their own left hand on their own left hip, still retaining hold of partner's right hand. Regain normal hold on step 6.
Note: Partners pass each other right shoulder to right shoulder.

Lady's steps

Preparatory Position: Start facing Centre, weight on **left foot**, in Double Hold. End facing Wall.

Step	Foot Position and Direction	Turn	Footwork	Body Alignment
1.	Tap **right foot** to side, along Line of Dance.	Nil.	Ball.	Facing Centre.
2.	Almost close **right foot** to **left foot**.	Nil.	Ball flat.	Facing Centre.
3.	Tap **left foot** to side, against Line of Dance.	Nil.	Ball.	Facing Centre.

4.	**Left foot** forward, to Centre.	Turning to right.	Heel flat.	Facing Centre.
5.	**Right foot** forward, diagonally to Centre.	Continue to turn.	Heel flat.	Facing diagonally to Centre.
6.	Close **left foot** to **right foot**.	½ to right, over steps 4-6.	Ball flat.	Facing Wall.

Rhythm: 1 – 2 – 3 – 4 – 5 – 6
Calling Cues: Tap – Step – Tap – Walk – Turn – Close
See note on hold following man's steps.

Loop Turn to Right

Man's steps

Preparatory Position: Start facing Wall, weight on **right foot**, in Double Hold.
End facing Centre.

Step	Foot Position and Direction	Turn	Footwork	Body Alignment
1.	Tap **left foot** to side, along Line of Dance.	Nil.	Ball.	Facing Wall.
2.	Almost close **left foot** to **right foot**.	Nil.	Ball flat.	Facing Wall.
3.	Tap **right foot** to side, against Line of Dance.	Nil.	Ball.	Facing Wall.
4.	**Right foot** forward, to Wall.	Turning to right.	Heel flat.	Facing Wall.
5.	**Left foot** forward, diagonally to Wall against Line of Dance.	Continue to turn.	Heel flat.	Facing diagonally to Wall against Line of Dance.
6.	Close **right foot** to **left foot**.	½ to right, over steps 4-6.	Ball flat.	Facing Centre.

Rhythm: 1 – 2 – 3 – 4 – 5 – 6
Calling Cues: Tap – Step – Tap – Walk – Turn – Close
Hold: The man raises the lady's right hand on step 3, releasing hold with his right hand. He then places the raised hands over the lady's head, over steps 4-5. Rejoin the hands to Double Hold on step 6.

Lady's steps

Preparatory Position: Start facing Centre, weight on **left foot**, in Double Hold. End facing Wall.

Step	Foot Position and Direction	Turn	Footwork	Body Alignment
1.	Tap **right foot.** to side, along Line of Dance.	Nil.	Ball.	Facing Centre.
2.	Almost close **right foot** to **left foot.**	Nil.	Ball flat.	Facing Centre.
3.	Tap **left foot** to side, against Line of Dance.	Nil.	Ball.	Facing Centre.
4.	**Left foot** forward, to Centre.	Turning to left.	Heel flat.	Facing Centre.
5.	**Right foot** to side, to Centre.	Continue to turn.	Ball flat.	Backing Line of Dance.
6.	Almost close **left foot** to **right foot.**	½ to left, over steps 4-6.	Ball flat.	Facing Wall.

Rhythm: 1 – 2 – 3 – 4 – 5 – 6
Calling Cues: Tap – Step – Tap – Walk – Turn – Close
Hold: The lady's right hand is raised on step 3, and her left hand is released. The raised hands are then placed over her head, over steps 4-5. Rejoin hands to Double Hold on step 6.

Arch Turn to Right

Man's steps

Preparatory Position: Start facing Wall, weight on **right foot**, in Double Hold. End facing Wall.

Step	Foot Position and Direction	Turn	Footwork	Body Alignment
1.	Tap **left foot** to side, along Line of Dance.	No turn, throughout.	Ball.	Facing Wall, throughout.
2.	Almost close **left foot** to **right foot.**		Ball flat.	
3.	Tap **right foot** to side, against Line of Dance.		Ball.	
4.	Almost close **right foot** to **left foot.**		Ball flat.	

| 5. | Replace weight to **left** foot, in place. | | Ball flat. | |
| 6. | Replace weight to **right** foot, in place. | | Ball flat. | |

Rhythm: 1 – 2 – 3 – 4 – 5 – 6
Calling Cues: Tap – Step – Tap – Step – Mark – Time
Hold: The man raises the lady's right hand on step 3, indicating to the lady, with his right hand, to turn to her right under the raised arms, he then releases hold. Rejoin the hands to Double Hold on step 6.

Lady's steps

Preparatory Position: Start facing Centre, weight on **left foot**, in Double Hold. End facing Centre.

Step	Foot Position and Direction	Turn	Footwork	Body Alignment
1.	Tap **right foot** to side, along Line of Dance.	Nil.	Ball.	Facing Centre.
2.	Almost close **right foot** to **left foot**.	Nil.	Ball flat.	Facing Centre.
3.	Tap **left foot** to side, against Line of Dance.	Nil.	Ball.	Facing Centre.
4.	**Left foot** forward and across **right foot**, down line of Dance.	Turning to right.	Heel flat.	Facing Line of Dance.
5.	Replace weight forward to **right foot**, in place.	Continue to turn.	Ball flat.	Facing diagonally to Wall against Line of Dance.
6.	Almost close **left foot** to **right foot**.	$\frac{1}{2}$ to right, over steps 4-6.	Ball flat.	Facing Centre.

Rhythm: 1 – 2 – 3 – 4 – 5 – 6
Calling Cues: Tap – Step – Tap – Walk – Turn – Close
Hold: The lady's right hand is raised on step 3, and her left hand is released. The lady then turns under the raised arms, over steps 4-5. Rejoin hands to Double Hold on step 6.

Arch Turn to Left

Man's steps

Preparatory Position: Start facing Wall, weight on **right foot**, in Double Hold. End facing Wall.

Step	Foot Position and Direction	Turn	Footwork	Body Alignment
1.	Tap **left foot** to side, along Line of Dance.	Nil.	Ball.	Facing Wall.
2.	Almost close **left foot** to **right foot**.	Nil.	Ball flat.	Facing Wall.
3.	Tap **right foot** to side, against Line of Dance.	Nil.	Ball.	Facing Wall.
4.	**Right foot** forward and across **left foot**, down line of Dance.	Turning to left.	Heel flat.	Facing Line of Dance.
5.	Replace weight forward to **left foot**, in place.	Continue to turn.	Ball flat.	Facing diagonally to Centre against Line of Dance.
6.	Almost close **right foot** to **left foot**.	½ to left, over steps 4-6.	Ball flat.	Facing Wall.

Rhythm: 1 – 2 – 3 – 4 – 5 – 6
Calling Cues: Tap – Step – Tap – Step – Turn – Close
Hold: The man raises the lady's right hand on step 3, releasing hold with the right hand. The man turns to the left under the raised arms, over steps 4-5. Re-join the hands to Double Hold on step 6.

Lady's steps

Preparatory Position: Start facing Centre, weight on **left foot**, in Double Hold. End facing Centre.

Step	Foot Position and Direction	Turn	Footwork	Body Alignment
1.	Tap **right foot** to side, along Line of Dance.	No turn, throughout.	Ball.	Facing Centre, throughout.
2.	Almost close **right foot** to **left foot**.		Ball flat.	
3.	Tap **left foot** to side, against Line of Dance.		Ball.	
4.	Almost close **left foot** to **right foot**.		Ball flat.	

| 5. | Replace weight to **right foot**, in place. | Ball flat. |
| 6. | Replace weight to **left foot**, in place. | Ball flat. |

Rhythm: 1 – 2 – 3 – 4 – 5 – 6
Calling Cues: Tap – Step – Tap – Step – Mark – Time
Hold: The lady's right hand is raised on step 3, her left hand is released. Rejoin the hands to Double Hold on step 6.

The Barrel Roll

Man's steps

Preparatory Position: Start facing Wall, weight on **right foot**, in Double Hold. End facing Wall.

Step	Foot Position and Direction	Turn	Footwork	Body Alignment
1-6.	Dance 1-6 of the Arch Turn to Left.	One complete turn to left.	As Arch Turn to Left.	As Arch Turn to Left.

Rhythm: 1 – 2 – 3 – 4 – 5 – 6
Calling Cues: Tap – Step – Tap – Step – Turn – Close
Hold: The man raises the lady's right hand on step 3, retaining hold with the right hand. The man turns to the left under the raised arms, over steps 4-5, bringing the joined right and lady's left hand down then up during the turn. The arms return to normal Double Hold on step 6.

Lady's steps

Preparatory Position: Start facing Centre, weight on **left foot**, in Double Hold. End facing Centre.

Step	Foot Position and Direction	Turn	Footwork	Body Alignment
1-6.	Dance 1-6 of the Arch Turn to Right.	One complete turn to right.	As Arch Turn to Right.	As Arch Turn to Right.

Rhythm: 1 – 2 – 3 – 4 – 5 – 6
Calling Cues: Tap – Step – Tap – Step – Turn – Close
Hold: The lady's right hand is raised on step 3. The lady then turns under the raised arms, over steps 4-5, retaining hold with the left hand, bringing the joined left and man's right hand down then up, during the turn. The arms return to normal Double Hold on step 6.

Note: During the turn the man and lady turn back-to-back.

The Wrap and Turn

Man's steps

Preparatory Position: Start facing Wall, weight on **right foot**, in Double Hold.
End facing Centre.

Step	Foot Position and Direction	Turn	Footwork	Body Alignment
1.	Tap **left foot** to side, along Line of Dance.	Nil.	Ball.	Facing Wall.
2.	Almost close **left foot** to **right foot**.	Nil.	Ball flat.	Facing Wall.
3.	Tap **right foot** to side, against Line of Dance.	Nil.	Ball.	Facing Wall.
4.	**Right foot** forward, to Wall.	Turning to right.	Heel flat.	Facing Wall.
5.	**Left foot** forward, against Line of Dance.	Continue to turn.	Heel flat.	Facing against Line of Dance.
6.	**Right foot** forward, to Centre.	½ turn to right, over steps 4-6.	Heel flat.	Facing Centre.
7.	**Left foot** forward, down line of Dance.	Continue to turn.	Heel flat.	Facing Line of Dance.
8.	**Right foot** forward, to Wall.	Continue to turn.	Heel flat.	Facing Wall.
9.	**Left foot** forward, against Line of Dance.	Continue to turn.	Heel flat.	Facing against Line of Dance.
10.	Replace weight to **right foot**, in place.	Continue to turn.	Ball flat.	Facing diagonally to Centre against Line of Dance.
11.	Replace weight to **left foot**, in place.	Continue to turn.	Ball flat.	Facing Centre.
12.	Replace weight to **right foot**, in place.	One complete turn to right, over steps 7-12.	Ball flat.	Facing Centre.

Rhythm: 1 – 2 – 3 – 4 – 5 – 6 – 7 – 8 – 9 – 10 – 11 – 12
Calling Cues: Tap – Step – Tap – Step – Turn – Turn – Turn – Turn – Check –
Rock – Rock – Rock
Hold: The man raises the lady's right hand on step 4, and lowers the joined hands
over the lady's head to finish in front of her body over steps 5-6. The man keeps

hold with his right hand with his arm behind the lady's back, the joined hands in front of the lady's body. On step 10, the man raises the joined left and right hands, keeping hold with his right hand to finish in Double Hold on step 12. *Note:* More or less turn can be made over the 12 steps.

Lady's steps

Preparatory Position: Start facing Centre, weight on **left foot**, in Double Hold. End facing Wall.

Step	Foot Position and Direction	Turn	Footwork	Body Alignment
1.	Tap **right foot** to side, along Line of Dance.	Nil.	Ball.	Facing Centre.
2.	Almost close **right foot** to **left foot**.	Nil.	Ball flat.	Facing Centre.
3.	Tap **left foot** to side, against Line of Dance.	Nil.	Ball.	Facing Centre.
4.	**Left foot** forward, to Centre.	Nil.	Heel flat.	Facing Centre.
5.	**Right foot** to side, a short step, along line of Dance.	Nil.	Ball flat.	Backing Wall.
6.	**Left foot** back, to Wall.	Nil.	Ball flat.	Backing Wall.
7.	**Right foot** back, against Line of Dance.	Turning strongly to right.	Ball flat.	Backing against Line of Dance.
8.	**Left foot** back, to Centre.	Turning strongly to right.	Ball flat.	Backing Centre.
9.	**Right foot** back, down line of Dance.	Turning strongly to right.	Ball flat.	Backing Line of Dance.
10.	**Left foot** back, a short step, down Line of Dance.	Turning strongly to right.	Ball flat.	Backing diagonally to Wall.
11.	**Right foot** forward, a short step, down Line of Dance.	Turning strongly to right.	Ball flat.	Facing Line of Dance.
12.	**Left foot** to side, a short step, along line of Dance.	One complete turn to right, over steps 7-12.	Ball flat.	Facing Wall.

Rhythm: 1 – 2 – 3 – 4 – 5 – 6 – 7 – 8 – 9 – 10 – 11 – 12
Calling Cues: Tap – Step – Tap – Step – Side – Back – Turn – Turn – Turn – Spin – Spin – Side
Hold: The lady's raises her right hand on step 4, and lowers the joined hands in front of her body, over steps 5-6. The lady retains hold with her left hand. On step 10, the lady raises her right hand, retaining hold with her left hand to finish in Double Hold on step 12.
Note: Steps 10-12 are very compact with the lady dancing the turn with little or no progression. More or less turn can be made over the 12 steps.

Disco Dances in Lines

'Line dancing' conjures up large groups all dancing fancy steps to country and western music. But there are several dances with a disco feel to them that come and go in popularity. In this short section, we present two dances – one that uses footwork and the other that mainly uses your hands and hips!

The Slosh

Preparatory Position: Man and Lady stand side by side, facing Wall.

Step	Foot Position and Direction	Turn	Footwork	Alignment
1.	**Left foot** to side, along Line of Dance.	Nil.	Ball flat, throughout	Facing Wall.
2.	Close **right foot** to **left foot.**	Nil.		Facing Wall.
3.	**Left foot** to side, along Line of Dance.	Nil.		Facing Wall.
4.	Kick **right foot** forward across **left foot.**	Nil.		Facing Wall.
5.	**Right foot** to side, against Line of Dance.	Nil.		Facing Wall.
6.	Close **left foot** to **right foot.**	Nil.		Facing Wall.
7.	**Right foot** to side, against Line of Dance.	Nil.		Facing Wall.

8.	Kick **left foot** across **right foot**.	Nil.		Facing Wall.
9 -12.	Repeat steps 1-4.	Nil.		Facing Wall.
13-15.	Repeat steps 5-7.	Nil.		Facing Wall.
16.	Flick **left foot** behind **right foot** and touch **left foot** with right hand.	Nil.		Facing Wall.
17.	Close **left foot** to **right foot**.	Turning to right make a ¼ of a turn, over steps 17-20.		Facing Wall.
18.	Raise **right foot** and touch right knee with right hand.			Facing Wall.
19.	Close **right foot** to **left foot**.			Facing Wall.
20.	Raise **left foot** and clap hands under left knee.			End facing against Line of Dance.

The Macarena

Yes, you really can make this dance look stylish! Add some hip movement to the basic arm movements and the dance flows smoothly: an excellent introduction to 'real' dancing to convince the doubters who think that they have two left feet!

Preparatory Position: Man and Lady stand side by side, facing Wall.

Step	Foot Position and Direction	Turn	Action	Body Alignment
1.	**Right arm** forward, palm down.	No turn, steps 1-14.	Hips right.	Facing Wall , steps 1-14.
2.	**Left arm** forward, palm down.		Hips left.	
3.	Turn **right palm** up.		Hips right.	
4.	Turn **left palm** up.		Hips left.	
5.	Place **right hand** on **left shoulder**.		Hips right.	

6.	Place **left hand** on **right shoulder**.		Hips left.	
7.	Place **right hand** over **right ear**.		Hips right.	
8.	Place **left hand** over **left ear**.		Hips left.	
9.	Place **right hand** on **left hip**.		Hips right.	
10.	Place **left hand** on **right hip**.		Hips left.	
11.	Place **right hand** behind **right hip**.		Hips right.	
12.	Place **left hand** behind **left hip**.		Hips left.	
13.	Rock to **right**.		Hips right.	
14.	Rock to **left**.		Hips left.	
15.	Jump.	Turn a ¼ to left.		Facing Line of Dance.

And that's it – the end of this book but, hopefully, just the start of your dancing enjoyment!

Suggested Music for Dancing

You may already have suitable music in your own music collection for practising the steps in this book. Disco and swing present no problems, but for the other dances here are a few suggestions; some of these are from Graham Beech, editor at Sigma Leisure, others from the kind people on the **rec.arts.dance** Internet news group. Some of the choices may seem surprising, some may not be to your liking, but they all work!

Waltz: Take It To The Limit *(The Eagles* or *Suzy Bogguss)*; If You Don't Know Me By Now *(Simply Red)*; Could I Have This Dance *(Anne Murray)*; Sam *(Olivia Newton-John)*; Love Ain't Here Anymore *(Take That)*; Give Me Forever *(John Tesh)*; I Wonder Why *(Curtis Stigers)*

Viennese (Quick) Waltz: After The Ball Is Over *(Nat King Cole)*; Dreams Of The Everyday Housewife *(Glen Campbell)*; Poisoning Pigeons In The Park *(Tom Lehrer)*; Skaters' Waltz *(Mantovani)*; Try Not To Breathe *(REM – on 'Automatic for The People')*

Social Foxtrot (slow): Lady In Red *(Chris de Burgh)*; Everything I Do *(Bryan Adams)*; almost anything by Frank Sinatra – e.g. (Love Is) The Tender Trap or It Happened in Monterey; Blue Moon and many, many more by Nat King Cole; numerous other artistes such as Manhattan Transfer or Harry Conick Jr.;

Social Foxtrot (fast): faster numbers by Frank Sinatra, Nat King Cole etc. Higher & Higher *(Jackie Wilson)*, also ideal for Quickstep.

Cha Cha Cha: Kokomo *(Beach Boys)*; Achy Breaky Heart *(Billy Ray Cyrus)*; All I Wanna Do *(Sheryl Crow)*; Hungry Eyes *(from Dirty Dancing)*; Re-light My Fire *(Take That)*; Oye Como Va *(Santana)*; Maria *(Brooks & Dunn)*;

Samba: Dancing Queen *(Abba)*; All That She Wants *(Ace of Base)*; Don't Talk Just Kiss *(Right Said Fred)*; Africa *(Toto)*; Love Is In The Air *(John Paul Young)*; La Isla Bonita *(Madonna)*; Live for Loving You *(Gloria Estefan)*

Rumba: Some Kind of Wonderful *(The Drifters)*; Sacrifice *(Elton John)*; Unbreak My Heart *(Toni Braxton)*; Perfidia (by Linda Ronstadt and others); I'm Not Letting You Go *(Gloria Estefan)*

Mambo/Salsa: Hey Mambo *(Barry Manilow)*; Just Help Yourself *(Tom Jones)*; I'm Going Bananas (Madonna); The Time Of My Life (Bill Medley & Jennifer Faires);Good Lovin' *(Kenny Ortega*, from the soundtrack of the film *Salsa;*several more on the soundtrack from 'The Mambo Kings' plus hundreds of albums, mostly by Cuban artists (e.g. Robert Pla on the Tumi record label).

Tango: Hernando's Hideaway (from 'The Pajama Game'); theme tune from "Phantom of The Opera"; I Want To Break Free *(Queen)*; Part Time Love *(Elton John)*

Merengue: relatively few popular songs – but try 'Tres Rei Momo' or 'Lie To Me' (David Byrne); also 'Tres Deseos' or 'Conga' *(Gloria Estefan)*. Hundreds of Cuban & South American recordings – see the notes on Salsa.

MORE BOOKS & CDs
FOR DANCING FEET!

LEARN TO DANCE: MODERN JIVE

This book & CD package is the only complete guide to Modern Jive - the fast and stylish partner dance also known as French-style Jive. It's a blend of jitterbug and rock 'n' roll that you can dance to music from fifties swing to today's chart hits! There are over 50 moves and 12 complete routines to make you the star of the dance floor! The authors are Robert Austin and Claire Hilliard, from the highly successful leJIVE organisation. **Price for book and CD: £10.95, POST FREE.**

START TO DANCE: MODERN JIVE

Recommended by Le Roc: the French Jive Chapter of the UKA professional dance teaching body. The 12-track CD has been specially engineered for jive dancing. It includes brand-new recordings from the gently-swinging "My Baby Just Cares For Me" to "Rhythm Is A Dancer" and "Just Can't Get Enough"! The booklet from the well-respected Le Roc organisation teaches you the basics of French Jive! In-store price: £9.95 **SPECIAL READER OFFER: £7.95**

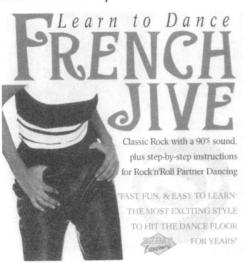

COUNTRY & WESTERN LINE DANCING FOR COWGIRLS & COWBOYS:
Step-by-Step Instructions

TOP VALUE BOOK & CD PACKAGE! This has been the number 1 best-selling line dance package in the UK since we launched it in 1996. Packed with 53 dances to the same high quality as UK LINE DANCE FAVOURITES and supplied with a FREE CD. **Just £12.95 for the complete package** - that's 24 pence per dance plus the pleasure of a top-quality CD of authentic C&W music!

UK LINE DANCE FAVOURITES:
Step-by-Step Instructions

The follow-up to the fastest-selling line dancing package in the UK- "Line Dancing for Cowgirls & Cowboys"- this new book and CD is crammed full with clear, tried and tested instructions for all the current UK favourites. It also features many new dances making the total number up to an amazing 52!

Its unique system of step-by-step, beat-by-beat instructions, makes it suitable for both beginners and experienced dancers. You will be guided in a carefully graded progression from the more simple to the most challenging of routines.

The book also gives suggestions for music and practising. (All the routines can be danced to the tracks on the first CD - available separately). **Price: £9.95**

ALL PRICES INCLUSIVE OF POSTAGE - ABSOLUTELY NO EXTRAS!
**We welcome VISA & MASTERCARD.
Orders to:
Sigma Leisure, 1 South Oak Lane, Wilmslow, Cheshire, SK9 6AR.
Tel: 01625-531035; Fax: 01625-536800
Our complete on-line catalogue is on the Internet:
http://www.sigmapress.co.uk**